A PUFFIN BOOK

PROPERTY OF

_____

_____

ADELINE YEN MAH's family considered her to be bad luck because her mother died giving birth to her. They discriminated against her and made her feel unwanted all her life. After the death of her stepmother in 1990, she felt compelled to write her story.

Falling Leaves became an international bestseller, and has been translated into many different languages. Drawing on her childhood as described in the early part of *Falling Leaves*, this book is the true story of Adeline Yen Mah's childhood up to the age of fourteen.

ADELINE YEN MAH
CHINESE CINDERELLA

PUFFIN

PUFFIN BOOKS

UK | USA | Canada | Ireland | Australia
India | New Zealand | South Africa

Puffin Books is part of the Penguin Random House group of companies whose
addresses can be found at global.penguinrandomhouse.com.

puffinbooks.com

First published in Australia by Penguin Books Ltd 1999
Published in Puffin Books 1999
Published in Puffin Modern Classics 2009
Reissued in this edition 2015

001

Text copyright © Adeline Yen Mah, 1999
All rights reserved

The moral right of the author has been asserted

Set in 12.5/16.5 pt Sabon LT Std
Typeset by Jouve (UK), Milton Keynes
Printed in Great Britain by Clays Ltd, St Ives plc

A CIP catalogue record for this book is available from the British Library

ISBN: 978-0-141-35941-0

www.greenpenguin.co.uk

MIX
Paper from
responsible sources
FSC® C018179

Penguin Random House is committed to a
sustainable future for our business, our readers
and our planet. This book is made from Forest
Stewardship Council® certified paper.

Dedicated to all unwanted children

I have always cherished this dream of creating something unique and imperishable, so that the past should not fade away forever. I know one day I shall die and vanish into the void, but hope to preserve my memories through my writing. Perhaps others who were also unwanted may see them a hundred years from now, and be encouraged. I imagine them opening the pages of my book and meeting me (as a ten-year-old) in Shanghai, without actually having left their own homes in Sydney, Tokyo, London, Hong Kong or Los Angeles. And I shall welcome each and every one of them with a smile and say, 'How splendid of you to visit me! Come in and let me share with you my story ... because I understand only too well the rankling in your heart and what you are going through.'

Acknowledgements

To my husband, Bob:
for putting up with me and for always being
there for me

To my children, Roger and Ann, and
my nephew, Gary:
for being proud of me

To my editor, Erica Wagner:
for her patient and skilful guidance

To my publisher, Bob Sessions:
for his belief in me

*For all of us to get along during this new
millennium we must understand each other's
history, language and culture. Towards that end
I am donating all royalties from* Falling Leaves
and Chinese Cinderella *to a foundation
modelled after the Rhodes Scholarship
programme to enable students to study at
universities in Beijing and Shanghai.*

Contents

Preface

Chinese Cinderella is my autobiography. It was difficult and painful to write but I felt compelled to do so. Though mine is but a simple, personal tale of my childhood, please do not underestimate the power of such stories. In one way or another, every one of us has been shaped and moulded by the stories we have read and absorbed in the past. All stories, including fairy-tales, present elemental truths which can sometimes permeate your inner life and become part of you.

The fact that this story is true may hold special appeal. Today, the world is a very different place. Though many Chinese parents still prefer sons, daughters are not so much despised. But the real things have not changed. It is still important to be truthful and loyal; to do the best you can; to make the most of your talents; to be happy with the simple things in life; and to believe deep down that you will ultimately triumph if you try hard enough to prove your worth.

To those who were neglected and unloved as children, I have a particular message. In spite of what your abusers would have had you believe, please be convinced that each of you has within you something precious and unique. *Chinese Cinderella* is dedicated to you with the fervent wish that you will persist in trying to do your best in the face of hopelessness; to have faith that in the end your spirit will prevail; to transcend your traumas and transform them into a source of courage, creativity and compassion.

Mother Teresa once said that 'loneliness and the feeling of being unwanted are the greatest poverty'. To this I will add: 'Please believe that one single positive dream is more important than a thousand negative realities.'

Adeline Yen Mah

Author's Note

Chinese is a pictorial language. Every word is a different picture and has to be memorised separately. There is no alphabet and no connection between the written and spoken language. A person can learn to read and write Chinese without knowing how to speak one word.

Because each word is a pictograph, Chinese calligraphy evokes a greater emotional response than the same word lettered in alphabet. The art of calligraphy is highly revered in China. Poetry written in calligraphy by ancient masters is prized and passed on from generation to generation.

Through *Chinese Cinderella*, I hope to intrigue you not only with the plight of a little girl growing up in China, but also interest you with her history and culture.

Names

In Chinese families, a child is called by many names.

1. My father's surname is Yen (嚴). My siblings and I inherited his surname of Yen (嚴). Chinese surnames come at the beginning of a person's name.
2. At birth, a baby is given a name by his or her parents. My given name is Jun-ling. Since my surname comes first, my Chinese name is Yen Jun-ling (嚴君玲).
3. At home, a child is called by a name dependent on the order of his or her birth. The oldest daughter is called Big Sister, the second daughter Second Sister and so on. There are separate Chinese words for 'older sister' (jie 姐) and 'younger sister' (mei 妹); 'older brother' (ge 哥) and 'younger brother' (di 弟). Since I was the fifth child in my family, my name at home was Fifth Younger Sister (Wu Mei 五妹). However, my younger siblings called me Wu Jie (五姐), which means 'Fifth Older Sister'.

4. When the older generation calls me Wu Mei (五妹) the word 'mei' takes on the meaning of 'daughter'. Wu Mei (五妹) now means Fifth Daughter.

5. The same goes for the word 'di'. Er Di (二弟) can mean Second Younger Brother or Second Son.

6. Our stepmother gave us European names when she married my father. When my brothers and I attended schools in Hong Kong and London where English was the main language, my name became Adeline Yen.

7. After I married, I adopted my Chinese American husband Bob Mah's last name and my name is now Adeline Yen Mah.

8. Big Sister's (大姐) name is Lydia, Big Brother's (大哥) is Gregory, Second Brother's (二哥) is Edgar, Third Brother's (三哥) is James. Fourth Younger Brother's name (四弟) is Franklin. Little Sister's name (小妹) is Susan.

1. Top of the Class
全 班 考 第 一

Autumn, 1941

AS SOON as I got home from school, Aunt Baba noticed the silver medal dangling from the left breast-pocket of my uniform. She was combing her hair in front of the mirror in our room when I rushed in and plopped my school-bag down on my bed.

'What's that hanging on your dress?'

'It's something special that Mother Agnes gave me in front of the whole class this afternoon. She called it an award.'

My aunt looked thrilled. 'So soon? You only started kindergarten one week ago. What is it for?'

'It's for topping my class this week. When Mother Agnes pinned it on my dress, she said I could wear it for seven days. Here, this certificate goes with it.' I opened my school-bag and handed her an envelope as I climbed onto her lap.

She opened the envelope and took out the certificate.

'Why, it's all written in French or English or some other foreign language. How do you expect me to read this, my precious little treasure?' I knew she was pleased because she was smiling as she hugged me. 'One day soon,' she continued, 'you'll be able to translate all this into Chinese for me. Until then, we'll just write today's date on the envelope and put it away somewhere safe. Go close the door properly and put on the latch so no one will come in.'

I watched her open her closet door and take out her safe-deposit box. She took the key from a gold chain around her neck and placed my certificate underneath her jade bracelet, pearl necklace and diamond watch – as if my award were also some precious jewel impossible to replace.

As she closed the lid, an old photograph fell out. I picked up the faded picture and saw a solemn young man and woman, both dressed in old-fashioned Chinese robes. The man looked rather familiar.

'Is this a picture of my father and dead mama?' I asked.

'No. This is the wedding picture of your grandparents. Your Ye Ye was twenty-six and your Nai Nai was only fifteen.' She quickly took the photo from me and locked it in her box.

'Do you have a picture of my dead mama?'

She avoided my eyes. 'No. But I have wedding pictures of your father and stepmother Niang. You were only one year old when they married. Do you want to see them?'

'No. I've seen those before. I just want to see one of my own mama. Do I look like her?' Aunt Baba did not reply, but busied herself putting the safe-deposit box back into her closet. After a while I said, 'When did my mama die?'

'Your mother came down with a high fever three days after you were born. She died when you were two weeks old . . .' She hesitated for a moment, then exclaimed suddenly, 'How dirty your hands are! Have you been playing in that sand-box at school again? Go wash them at once! Then come back and do your homework!'

I did as I was told. Though I was only four years old, I understood I should not ask Aunt Baba too many questions about my dead mama. Big Sister once told me, 'Aunt Baba and Mama used to be best friends. A long time ago, they worked together in a bank in Shanghai owned by our Grand Aunt, the youngest sister of Grandfather Ye Ye. But then Mama died giving birth to you. If you had not been born, Mama would still be alive. She died because of you. You are bad luck.'

2. A Tianjin Family
天 津 家 庭

AT THE time of my birth, Big Sister was six and a half years old. My three brothers were five, four and three. They blamed me for causing Mama's (媽媽) death and never forgave me.

A year later, Father (爸爸) remarried. Our stepmother, whom we called Niang (娘), was a seventeen-year-old Eurasian beauty fourteen years his junior. Father always introduced her to his friends as his French wife though she was actually half French and half Chinese. Besides Chinese, she spoke French and English. She was almost as tall as Father, stood very straight and dressed only in French clothes – many of which came from Paris. Her thick, wavy, black hair never had a curl out of place. Her large, dark-brown eyes were fringed with long, thick lashes. She wore heavy make-up, expensive French perfume and many diamonds and pearls. It was Grandmother Nai Nai who told us to call her Niang, another Chinese term for 'mother'.

One year after their wedding, they had a son (Fourth Brother) followed by a daughter (Little Sister). There were now seven of us: five children from Father's first wife and two from our stepmother, Niang.

As well as Father and Niang, we lived with our Grandfather Ye Ye (爺爺), Grandmother Nai Nai (奶奶) and Aunt Baba (姑媽) in a big house in the French Concession of Tianjin, a city port on the north-east coast of China. Aunt Baba was the older sister of our father. Because she was meek, shy, unmarried and had no money of her own, my parents ordered her to take care of me. From an early age, I slept in a cot in her room. This suited me well because I grew to know her better and better and we came to share a life apart from the rest of our family. Under the circumstances, perhaps it was inevitable that, in time, we loved each other very deeply.

Many years before, China had lost a war (known as the Opium War) against England and France. As a result, many coastal cities in China (such as Tianjin and Shanghai) came to be occupied by foreign soldiers.

The conquerors parcelled out the best areas of these treaty ports for themselves, claiming them as their own 'territories' or 'concessions'. Tianjin's French Concession was like a little piece of Paris transplanted into the centre of this big Chinese city. Our house was built in the French style and looked as if it had been lifted from a tree-shaded avenue near the Eiffel Tower. Surrounded by a charming garden, it had porches, balconies, bow windows, awnings and a slanting tile roof. Across the street was St Louis Catholic Boys' School, where the teachers were French missionaries.

In December 1941, when the Japanese bombed Pearl Harbor, the United States became involved in the Second World War. Although Tianjin was occupied by the Japanese, the French Concession was still being governed by French officials. French policemen strutted about looking important and barking out orders in their own language, which they expected everyone to understand and obey.

At my school, Mother Agnes taught us the alphabet and how to count in French. Many of the streets around our house were named after dead French heroes or Catholic saints. When translated into Chinese, these street names became so complicated that Ye Ye and Nai Nai often had trouble remembering them. Bilingual store signs were common but the most exclusive shops painted their signs only in French. Nai Nai told us this was the foreigners' way of announcing that no Chinese were allowed there except for maids in charge of white children.

3. Nai Nai's Bound Feet
奶奶的小脚

THE DINNER-BELL rang at seven. Aunt Baba took my hand and led me into the dining-room.

My grandparents were just ahead of us. Aunt Baba told me to run quickly to the head of the big, round dining-table and pull out Grandmother Nai Nai's chair for her. Nai Nai walked very slowly because of her bound feet. I watched her as she inched her way towards me, hobbling and swaying as if her toes had been partly cut off. As she sat down with a sigh of relief, I placed my foot next to her embroidered, black-silk shoe to compare sizes.

'Nai Nai, how come your feet are so tiny?' I asked.

'When I was three years old, a tight bandage was wound around my feet, bending the toes under the sole and crushing the arch so that my feet would remain small all my life. This has been the custom in China for over one thousand years, ever since the Tang dynasty. In my day, small feet were considered feminine and beautiful. If you had large and unbound feet, no man would marry you. This was the custom.'

'Did it hurt?'

'Of course! It hurt so badly I couldn't sleep. I screamed with pain and begged my mother to free my feet but she wouldn't. In fact, the pain has never gone away. My feet have hurt every day since they were bound and continue to hurt today. I had a pair of perfectly normal feet when I was born, but they maimed me on purpose and gave me life-long arthritis so I would be attractive. Just be thankful this horrible custom was done away with thirty years ago. Otherwise your feet would be crippled and you wouldn't be able to run or jump either.'

I went to the foot of the table and sat at my assigned seat between Second Brother and Third

Brother as my three brothers ran in, laughing and jostling each other. I cringed as Second Brother sat down on my right. He was always saying mean things to me and grabbing my share of goodies when nobody was looking.

Second Brother used to sit next to Big Brother but the two of them fought a lot. Father finally separated them when they broke a fruit bowl fighting over a pear.

Big Brother winked at me as he sat down. He had a twinkle in his eye and was whistling a tune. Yesterday he'd tried to teach me how to whistle but no matter how hard I tried I couldn't make it work. Was Big Brother up to some new mischief today? Last Sunday afternoon, I came across him crouched by Grandfather Ye Ye's bed, watching him like a cat while Ye Ye took his nap. A long black hair from Ye Ye's right nostril was being blown out and drawn in with every snore. Silently but swiftly, Big Brother suddenly approached Ye Ye and carefully pinched the nasal hair between his forefinger and thumb. There was a tantalising pause as Ye Ye exhaled with a long, contented wheeze. Meanwhile I held my breath, mesmerised and not daring to make a sound. Finally, Ye Ye inhaled deeply. Doggedly, Big Brother hung on.

The hair was wrenched from its root. Ye Ye woke up with a yell, jumped from his bed, took in the situation with one glance and went after Big Brother with a feather duster. Laughing hysterically, Big Brother rushed out of the room, slid down the banister and made a clean getaway into the garden, all the time holding Ye Ye's hair aloft like a trophy.

Third Brother took his seat on my left. His lips were pursed and he was trying to whistle unsuccessfully. Seeing the medal on my uniform, he raised his eyebrow and smiled at me. 'What's that?' he asked.

'It's an award for topping my class. My teacher says I can wear it for seven days.'

'Congratulations! First week at school and you get a medal! Not bad!'

While I was basking in Third Brother's praise, I suddenly felt a hard blow across the back of my head. I turned around to see Second Brother glowering at me.

'What did you do *that* for?' I asked angrily.

Deliberately, he took my right arm under the table and gave it a quick, hard twist while no one was looking. 'Because I feel like it, that's why, you

ugly little squirt! This'll teach you to show off
your medal!'

I turned for help from Third Brother but he
was looking straight ahead, obviously not wishing
to be involved. At that moment, Father, Niang
and Big Sister came in together and Second
Brother immediately let go of my arm.

Niang was speaking to Big Sister in English and
Big Sister was nodding assent. She glanced at
all of us smugly as she took her seat between
Second Brother and Niang, full of her own
self-importance at being so favoured by our
stepmother. Because her left arm had been
paralysed from a birth injury, her movements
were slow and awkward and she liked to order
me, or Third Brother, to carry out her chores.

'Wu Mei (Fifth Younger Sister)!' she now said.
'Go fetch my English–Chinese dictionary. It's on
my bed in my room. Niang wants me to translate
something . . .'

I was halfway off my chair when Nai Nai said,
'Do the translation later! Sit down, Wu Mei. Let's
have dinner first before the dishes get cold. Here,
let me first pick a selection of soft foods to send
up to the nursery so the wet nurse can feed the

two youngest . . .' She turned to Niang with a smile. 'Another two years and all seven grandchildren will be sitting around this table. Won't that be wonderful?'

Niang's two-year-old son, Fourth Brother, and her infant daughter, Little Sister, were still too young to eat with us. However, they were already 'special' from the moment of their birth. Though nobody actually said so, it was simply understood that everyone considered Niang's 'real' children to be better-looking, smarter, and simply superior in every way to Niang's stepchildren. Besides, who dared disagree?

For dessert, the maids brought in a huge bowl of my favourite fruit, dragons' eyes! I was so happy I couldn't help laughing out loud.

Nai Nai gave us each a small bowl of fruit and I counted seven dragons' eyes in mine. I peeled off the leathery brown skin and was savouring the delicate white flesh when Father suddenly pointed to my medal.

'Is this medal for topping your class?' he asked.

I nodded eagerly, too excited to speak. A hush fell upon the table. This was the first time anyone could remember Father singling me out or saying anything to me. Everyone looked at my medal.

'Is the left side of your chest heavier?' Father continued, beaming with pride. 'Are you tilting?'

I flushed with pleasure and could barely swallow. My big Dia Dia was actually teasing me! On his way out, he even patted me on my head. Then he said, 'Continue studying hard and bringing honour to our Yen family name so we can be proud of you.'

All the grown-ups beamed at me as they followed Father out of the room. How wonderful! My triumph had become Father's triumph! I must study harder and keep wearing this medal so I can go on pleasing Father, I thought to myself.

But what was this? Big Sister was coming towards me with a scowl. Without a word, she reached over and snatched two dragons' eyes from my bowl as she left the room. My three brothers followed her example. Then they all ran out, leaving me quite alone with my silver medal, staring at my empty bowl.

4. Life in Tianjin
天 津 生 活

A few months later in early 1942. Winter-time

WHEN I started kindergarten at St Joseph's French Convent School, Big Sister had been going there for years and years and was already in the fifth grade. She complained so much about having to walk me to and from school that Grandmother Nai Nai finally told Ah Mao, the rickshaw-puller, to take us there and back.

Father had bought the black, shiny rickshaw three years earlier as a fiftieth birthday present for Nai Nai to visit her friends and play mahjong. It had inflatable rubber tyres, a brass lamp on each side and a bell operable by foot as well as by hand. Every morning, Ah Mao could be seen sweeping the seat, washing the sides, brushing the canopy and polishing the brass. My brothers were forever begging him to let them pull each other back and forth in the garden but Ah Mao was fiercely protective and would scatter them away.

Outside our garden, an old, blind and crippled beggar-woman often sat on the pavement. As soon as Ah Mao opened the gate, she would bang her tin plate, tilt back her head and wail in a loud voice, 'Have pity on me!' Big Sister (Da Jie 大姐) and I were both a little frightened of her. 'Run faster!' Big Sister would urge Ah Mao. 'Get away from her as fast as you can!'

I was always happy when our rickshaw approached the imposing red brick building of St Joseph's. I loved everything about my school: all the other little girls dressed in identical white starched uniforms just like mine; the French Franciscan nuns in black and white habits with big metal crosses dangling from their necks; learning numbers, the catechism and the alphabet; playing hopscotch and skipping at recess. My classmates made me feel like I belonged. Unlike my siblings, nobody looked down on me.

The school-bell rang and it was time to go home. I rushed out of the classroom and ran straight towards Ah Mao, who was smoking a cigarette and squatting on his haunches between the handlebars of his rickshaw on the pavement by the school gate. He smiled as I approached and waved me into his cab.

'I wonder how long we're going to have to wait today,' he grumbled as he lit a fresh cigarette.

I said nothing but I knew what he meant. It *was* annoying. Big Sister was always among the last to leave when school finished. She seemed to enjoy having her friends notice that her rickshaw-puller and younger sister could be found waiting for her every afternoon while she took her own sweet time.

Today we waited even longer than usual. It was beastly cold and there was a sharp north-westerly wind blowing. After a while Ah Mao wandered off to chat with a tea-pedlar on the corner and warm his hands against the pedlar's steaming kettle. My face, fingers and toes were numb with cold.

Finally, I saw Big Sister appear in the playground, laughing and joking with a few big girls from her class until the nuns shooed them out and locked the gate behind them. Big Sister scowled as she climbed in, while I shrank into my corner. She jabbed the bell angrily several times with her foot and called sharply. Ah Mao ran back, stepped between the shafts and off we went.

'What did the nuns teach you today?' Big Sister suddenly asked imperiously.

'They taught us about God,' I replied proudly.

'I'm going to test you. Who made you?'

I was happy because I knew the answer. 'God made me.'

'Why did God make you?'

'I don't know, because Teacher hasn't told us yet.'

'That's just an excuse!' Big Sister screamed. 'You don't know because you are stupid! And you don't deserve to wear this!' Suddenly, she grabbed my medal and jerked it, becoming enraged because I was pushing her away. 'Take that! Medal-winner! Teacher's pet! Who do you think you are? Showing off week after week!' Big Sister cried as she slapped me with her strong right hand.

Ah Mao, who had stopped at a red light, turned around to look when he heard the slap. Big Sister nonchalantly straightened her uniform, ordering him to run faster because she was hungry. She told Ah Mao that Cook was making pot-stickers and they were her favourite afternoon snack. As soon as we were home, Big Sister jumped down and ran off. Ah Mao helped me alight, pointed to my medal, smiled broadly, and gave me the thumbs-up sign, shaking his fist up and down to signal his admiration.

I was winning the medal every week and wearing it constantly. I knew this displeased my siblings, especially Big Sister and Second Brother, but it was the only way to make Father take notice and be proud of me. Besides, my teachers and schoolmates seemed to be happy for me. I loved my school more and more.

Finally, it was the end of term. Our whole school was assembled in the auditorium for prize-giving. The French Monsignor himself was waiting on stage to present us with awards. Mother Agnes suddenly called my name in front of everyone. She announced that I had won a special award for wearing the weekly medal for more weeks than any other student. My heart beat wildly as I approached the stage, but the steps leading up to the Monsignor were too high and steep for my short little legs. What should I do? Finally, I had no choice but to climb up to the stage on my hands and knees. Everyone was hooting with laughter and clapping wildly. Were they applauding me?

On my way back to my seat, I couldn't help noticing that of all the prize-winners, I was the only one unaccompanied by anyone from my family. Nobody was there to pat my head or congratulate me, not even my Aunt Baba. As for Big Sister, she had refused to go to school that day. She'd said she had a stomach-ache.

Aunt Baba told me that Japan was a strong country which had conquered most of China, including the city of Tianjin where we lived. My three brothers were always grumbling about the Japanese classes they were required to take at school. We children were supposed to show our respect and bow whenever we ran past Japanese soldiers. Otherwise they would punish us or even kill us. Once, Big Brother's best friend was kicked and slapped by a Japanese soldier because he forgot to bow when he ran past him. Another time, Ye Ye stopped Third Brother from kicking a ball made of old newspapers because a photo of the Japanese emperor was visible on its surface. Everyone hated the Japanese, but even the grown-ups were scared of them. Now there was talk that the Japanese were demanding to become Father's business partners.

Father looked terribly worried and his hair started to fall out. Many Japanese men in business suits came to the house looking for Father, even on Sundays. They came with Japanese bodyguards who wore surgical masks on their faces and carried scary-looking bayonets with big, sharp knives at the tips. It was a great nuisance because we had to bow and show respect to anyone who looked Japanese. After their departure, Father would talk to Ye Ye for hours and hours, in their office.

One morning, Father left the house to buy stamps at the post office down the road. He never came home.

Ye Ye reported Father's disappearance to the police. He put up posters and placed advertisements in the newspapers offering a reward for news of Father's whereabouts, alive or dead. The Japanese came back a few times looking for Father but soon lost interest. With Father absent, his business ground to a halt. There was no more money to be made and the Japanese dropped their demands.

A few months later, our stepmother Niang took our younger brother (Fourth Brother) and left the house also. Nobody knew where they had gone. It was all rather frightening and very mysterious.

Ye Ye told us that Father, Niang and Fourth Brother had left for a while. After the strangeness wore off, we weren't particularly bothered because Father often travelled on business. Besides, Ye Ye, Nai Nai and Aunt Baba were still home. The Japanese stopped bothering us. Life settled down and became tranquil, even happy.

Ye Ye employed seven maids, a cook, a chauffeur and Ah Mao, the rickshaw-puller. The grown-ups held frequent mah-jong parties. We children could invite our friends home to play. On Sundays, Ye Ye took everyone out for drives in Father's big black motorcar. We lunched at different restaurants in the foreign Concessions – French, Russian, German, Italian and Japanese. Sometimes, we even saw movies suitable for children! Life seemed better than ever.

*

Father, Niang and Fourth Brother had been gone for well over a year and I had almost forgotten them. There was a heatwave on and we were all in the parlour discussing the next day's dinner menu. Aunt Baba suggested to Cook that we should have dumplings instead of rice for a change. Those yummy dumplings were stuffed with pork, chives and spring onions and were absolutely delicious! Big Brother shouted that he could eat fifty of them at one sitting. Second Brother immediately claimed sixty and Third Brother wanted sixty also. Big Sister ordered seventy. Big Brother told her she was already too fat. She screamed at him to shut up and they started to argue.

Nai Nai said, 'What a racket! I'm getting a headache from all this commotion. It's getting late. I'm going to my room to soak my aching feet.' She turned to me. 'Wu Mei! Run down to the kitchen and tell them to bring me a pan of hot water.'

I watched the maid pour the steaming hot water from a thermos flask into an enamel basin and followed her into Nai Nai's bedroom. Nai Nai was sitting on the edge of her bed, slowly unwinding the filmy silk bindings from her feet. 'Are you sure you want to stay here?' she asked me. 'Your Nai Nai's feet are going to stink up this room as soon as I take these bindings off.'

'Please let me stay!' I begged as I squatted beside her on the floor. The truth was that I was fascinated by her tiny feet. It was like watching a horror movie: you want to see it and not see it at the same time.

I stared at Nai Nai's toes, all deformed and twisted grotesquely beneath her soles. Slowly she immersed them in the pan of hot water, sighing with relief and contentment. She then rubbed them gently with a bar of sweet-smelling soap until the whole basin was covered with lather. Aunt Baba came in and helped Nai Nai trim her thick toe-nails and cut off pieces of dead skin. 'See how lucky you are?' Nai Nai said to me. 'By being born at the right time, both you and your Aunt Baba didn't have to go through the torture I suffered in having my feet bound. How I wish I could have just one day when my feet didn't hurt!'

'When Nai Nai was your age, she already couldn't run or jump any more!' Aunt Baba said to me. 'And here you even get to go to school every day just like your brothers. You'd better run along now and go to bed! It's way past your bedtime.'

After I left, Aunt Baba talked to Nai Nai for a little while longer. She then went to take her bath.

Fifteen minutes later, Ye Ye was pounding on her bathroom door. Nai Nai had fainted and was frothing at the mouth. Aunt Baba telephoned the doctor but it was already too late. Nai Nai had died of a massive stroke.

I woke up from a sound sleep and saw Aunt Baba sitting by herself at the dressing-table and crying. I crawled into her lap and put my arms around her to comfort her. Aunt Baba told me that Nai Nai's life had evaporated like an episode of a spring dream. Outside, I could hear the crickets humming in the summer heat and hawkers shouting their wares on the pavement below. How could everything remain so much the same when Nai Nai was no longer with us?

Nai Nai's body was placed in a tightly sealed coffin in the parlour. Buddhist monks dressed in long robes chanted their mantras. Ye Ye ordered us children to spend the night and sleep on the floor in the same room to keep Nai Nai company. Third Brother whispered in my ear that Nai Nai was going to push open the coffin lid and wander out at midnight. I was scared and couldn't sleep. All night, while listening to the monks praying and watching their shining bald heads in the flickering candle-light, I half yearned and half feared that Nai Nai would crawl out and resume her place among us.

Next day, there was a grand funeral. Nai Nai's coffin was draped with white sheets and placed on a hearse pulled by four men. We all dressed in white robes with white headbands for the boys and white ribbons for the girls. Big Brother acted as chief mourner in Father's absence. Hired professional musicians extolled Nai Nai's virtues. They tossed white paper coins into the air while making music and singing prayers. The hearse stopped six times for Big Brother to fall to his knees, kowtow and bewail Nai Nai's loss in a loud voice.

At the Buddhist Temple, the monks held a solemn ceremony. Amidst hymns and the scent of incense, we burned sundry articles made of paper for Nai Nai's needs in the next world. There were cardboard beds, tables, chairs, pots and pans and even a mah-jong set. My brothers fought over a large paper car covered with bright tin foil. I watched the smoke curl up from the sacrificial urn and believed with all my heart that it would regroup somewhere in heaven into useful household utensils for the exclusive use of our Nai Nai.

5. Arrival in Shanghai
到 達 上 海

SIX WEEKS after Nai Nai's funeral, Ye Ye took Big Sister, Big Brother, Second Brother and me for an outing. To our surprise, our car stopped first at the railroad station. After instructing our chauffeur to wait outside in the car, Ye Ye marched the four of us onto a crowded platform marked with a sign 'To Shanghai'. There, in a first-class compartment, we came face to face with Father, sitting by himself. He was dressed in a black suit and black tie. His eyes were red and he had been crying.

We were delighted and astonished. Big Sister asked, 'How long have you been back, Father?' He told her he had just arrived a few hours ago but was planning to leave again almost immediately. He said he missed us and was in Tianjin specially to escort us south to Shanghai. He told us Shanghai was a large port city one thousand miles away and our Grand Aunt owned a big bank there. Father, Niang and Fourth Brother had been living there for one and a half years. Since Third Brother was still recuperating from measles, he would join us later with Little Sister, Ye Ye and Aunt Baba. Being devout Buddhists, Ye Ye and Aunt Baba wished to observe the traditional hundred-day religious mourning-period for Nai Nai before leaving Tianjin.

'What about our clothes?' Big Brother asked.

'Aunt Baba is arranging to have them delivered separately,' Father replied. 'If you had taken too much luggage with you, the servants would have become suspicious. It's important that the servants know nothing about my whereabouts. Otherwise, the Japanese might arrest me. During the train journey, talk to each other as little as possible so you'll give nothing away. Now, say goodbye to your Ye Ye! The train is leaving in five minutes!'

Father's Shanghai house was situated on Avenue Joffre, deep in the heart of the French Concession.

It was a big, square, dark-grey concrete building, just like all the other sixty-nine houses within the same 'long tang', a cluster of houses surrounded by a communal wall. Father's chauffeur drove us from the station through the main lane of our 'long tang', turned left into a narrower alleyway, and stopped in front of a wrought-iron gate. Father led us into a charming garden, with a small lawn lined by clipped camellia bushes, a magnolia tree with wonderfully fragrant blooms, and a wishing-well next to a wooden dog-house. A large, ferocious-looking German Shepherd rushed out, jumped excitedly at the sight of Father, but barked at us. I glanced briefly at the large, brutish animal with its sharp teeth and pointed ears. Father noticed and said to me, 'His name is Jackie. Don't be afraid of him. Just behave naturally. He is getting obedience training lessons every week from a German dog-trainer. He won't dare bite you.'

All the same, I was nervous. I got away and followed Big Brother up three stone steps through tall French doors into the formal living-room.

'Here we are!' Father said, looking around proudly as we gawked in open-mouthed wonder at the burgundy-red velvet couches, matching velvet curtains and thick woollen carpet partially covering a teak parquet floor. The wallpaper had long strips of raised velvet napping which matched the curtains. Beautiful white orchids in an antique Ming Dynasty vase rested on an elegant imitation Louis XVI coffee-table. Everything was ornate, formal, polished and hard.

Niang entered, holding Fourth Brother's hand. We greeted her timidly. Like the room, our stepmother was stylish and flawless with her large, piercing eyes, long shapely nails painted bright red, and enormous flashing diamonds at her throat, wrist and ears. Standing opposite her made me feel quite shabby and ill at ease.

'Sit down, all of you! And welcome to our Shanghai home!' Niang announced in a loud, clear voice. 'The maids will show you to your rooms. This house consists of three floors. On the ground floor, the living-room and dining-room are in the front. The kitchen, garage and servants' quarters are at the back. You are to enter and leave the house by the back door only. The front gate leading out of the garden is reserved for your father's guests. So is the living-room. You are not to invite any of your friends home, or to visit them in their houses.

'The first floor is where your father and I, and your younger brother and sister, have our rooms.

You are not allowed to enter any of the rooms on our floor without our permission.

'All of you will live on the second floor. You three boys will sleep in the same room. Wu Mei (Fifth Daughter) will share a room with Aunt Baba. Ye Ye and Big Sister will each have a private room. Keep your rooms tidy because your father and I might come up and make an inspection at any time.

'We have enrolled all of you at very expensive private missionary schools. School starts next Monday. Now go with the maids to your rooms and wash yourselves. In half an hour, Cook will ring the dinner-bell. As soon as you hear it, all of you will come down at once. Do you understand?'

We nodded solemnly. As we climbed the stairs, Big Brother muttered, 'To her, we are not separate people. Over here, we have become one single unit known as *all of you*. Seems like this is how it's going to be from now on.'

6. First Day at School
第 一 天 上 學

ON MONDAY morning, with Aunt Baba still in Tianjin, a maid helped me put on my brand-new school uniform. It was a little too long, stiff with starch, white in colour and had the name of my new school, Sacred Heart (Sheng Xin 聖心), in bright-red Chinese characters embroidered on the left breast-pocket.

After breakfast, I stood in the hallway for what seemed like a very long time waiting for someone to take me to school, wondering who it was going to be. I was excited to be starting first grade in my new primary school, which was located next door to Big Sister's Aurora Middle School. Big Sister, however, was still in bed. Her classes were scheduled to begin one hour later than mine. The chauffeur had already left to drive my brothers to St John's Academy, which was in the opposite direction.

I saw Cook wheeling his bicycle through the hallway to go to market. Now he spotted me watching him.

'Who is taking you to school?' he asked.

'I don't know.' I was nervous and couldn't help shooting a wistful glance at the big clock ticking away on the wall. It was getting late and everyone had forgotten about me. What should I do? I was becoming panic-stricken and felt tears rolling down my cheeks.

Cook shrugged. 'It's certainly not *my* job. No one mentioned anything to me about you.' He was about to mount his bike and ride away when he noticed my tears. 'Now, now! Don't cry! Being late for school isn't the end of the world . . . Oh, all right! Come along then!' he mumbled gruffly as he lifted me onto the handlebar of his bicycle. 'Your Sheng Xin Primary School happens to be right next to the market. Sit here quietly and don't squirm. We'll be there in no time at all.'

After school was let out in the early afternoon, I waited with all the other first-graders by the school gate. One by one they were greeted and led away by their anxiously hovering mothers. Eventually, I was the only one left. Nobody had come for me. The metal gate slowly clanged shut behind me as I watched my classmates disperse, each clutching her mother's hand and eagerly recounting the adventures of her first day at school. After a long time, I peered through a crack into the deserted playground. Not a person was in sight. Cautiously, I pushed against the massive iron gate. It was firmly locked. Trembling with fear, I realised that nobody was coming to pick me up. Too embarrassed to knock or draw attention to myself, I walked out tentatively into the Shanghai streets. Surely, if I tried hard enough, I would remember the way home.

It was a beautiful, sunny afternoon. At first I wandered along a wide, straight road lined with tall, leafy trees. Motor cars, trams, rickshaws, pedicabs and bicycles whizzed by. I kept walking but dared not cross the road, glancing briefly at the open-fronted stores overhung with colourful, upright, bilingual signboards. I turned a corner and now the pavements seethed with people and noise and commotion: coolies shouldering heavy loads on bamboo poles; hawkers selling toys, crickets in cages, fans, cold tea, candies, meat-filled buns, spring rolls, tea-eggs and fermented bean curd; stalls and booths offering services such as hair-cuts, shaves, dental care, letter-writing, extraction of ear wax; beggars banging tin cups and chanting for a handout. Except for me, everyone was striding along purposefully, going somewhere. Everyone had a destination. I must have walked for miles and miles. But where was I?

Should I enter a shop and ask for directions? But I didn't know my home address. What should I say? Should I approach that kindly old storekeeper smiling at me from the doorway of his antique shop and tell him, 'Please, sir, I want to go home.' But, where *was* my home?

It was getting dark. Bright neon signs in blue, yellow, red and orange came on and were blinking at me. Had anyone at home missed me? Did they think I was still at school? Were they looking for me? What should I do?

I walked past a bustling, brightly lit dim sum shop. Such a wonderful aroma was wafting through the door! Through the plate-glass window, I saw roast ducks, soya-sauce chickens, and hunks of glistening roast pork hanging from hooks. There was a young chef wielding his cleaver and deftly chopping a duck into bite-sized pieces on a wooden block. Wouldn't it be heavenly to be given a slice of meat? But that might be too much to hope for. I would be quite content with a piece of bone to chew on. As I salivated, I imagined the taste of the food sliding down my throat. Breakfast seemed such a long time ago!

Someone was touching my shoulder. I started and looked up. A large, red-faced woman whom I had just seen bustling around the tables in the restaurant was speaking to me. 'You have been standing here for almost half an hour. What's your mother doing that she would leave you waiting out here all by yourself? Doesn't she know it's dangerous for a little girl your age to be hanging around on the street like this? Are you supposed to have dinner with her here?'

Terrified, I lowered my head and shuffled my feet. 'Come and wait for her inside,' she commanded as she glanced at my brand-new school uniform. 'My daughter started school today too.'

Inside, it was hot and noisy. I stood hesitantly by the door. Suddenly, I noticed a black telephone next to the cash register! Why, just yesterday, Big Brother and I were playing and he taught me a new 'numbers' game he had just invented. 'Take any number and add, subtract, multiply, or divide it. The one who first comes up with number 13 wins!'

'What number should we use, Big Brother?' I had asked.

'Run downstairs and get our telephone number,' he'd said. 'It's marked on the front of the telephone in the stairway.'

I'd rushed down for the number and we'd played with it all afternoon: backwards and forwards, breaking it down and building it up again. 79281! That was it! 79281!

Finally, Big Brother had won! He'd broken 79281 into 9, 8, 21 and 7:

$$9 - 8 = 1$$
$$21 \div 7 = 3$$

He'd then placed the number 3 to the right of the number 1 and got 13, thereby winning the game. I had clapped my hands in glee and admiration. I felt honoured that Big Brother had deigned to play with me all afternoon.

No one was looking when I picked up the phone and dialled. Father answered on the third ring.

'Speak up!' Father was shouting. 'There is so much background noise. Who is it?'

'It's your daughter, Fifth Daughter (Wu Mei 五妹).'

'Where are you?' Father asked in an even voice, quite calmly; and, suddenly, with a pang, I realised that nobody had missed me. They didn't even know I wasn't home.

'I'm in a restaurant. I got lost when I tried to walk home from school.'

'Let me speak to the proprietor. You stay right there and I'll come and pick you up.'

Soon afterwards, Father arrived and drove me home in his big black Buick. Traffic was light and he drove in silence. When we arrived, he patted me on my head. 'Next time you go anywhere for the first time,' he admonished as he handed me a map of Shanghai from the glove compartment of his car, 'read this map and find where you are and where you wish to go. This way you'll never get lost again.'

That's exactly what I'll do, I thought to myself. After dinner, I'm going to ask Big Brother to teach me how to read this map. With Aunt Baba still in Tianjin, there's obviously nobody looking out for me. I'll just have to find my own way.

7. Family Reunion
全 家 團 聚

BIG BROTHER told me that Ye Ye, Aunt Baba, Third Brother and Little Sister were scheduled to arrive in Shanghai on the last Sunday in October. I started counting the days. Little Sister had been separated from her mother Niang since she was only six months old. Now she was almost two and Aunt Baba mentioned in her last letter that Little Sister was starting to jabber away in Mandarin with a strong Tianjin accent. How adorable!

On the morning of their arrival, Father and the chauffeur met them at the station. I was overjoyed to see my beloved Aunt Baba and Ye Ye again. Third Brother looked taller and thinner but Little

Sister had changed the most. Aunt Baba had dressed her in pretty pink silk trousers with a matching jacket and pink cloth shoes. Her hair was neatly combed into two little beribboned plaits which stood up on each side, bobbing as she walked. She looked like a big doll with her large round eyes and chubby pink cheeks, rushing around the sitting-room, examining the dishes of candy, melon seeds, peanuts, ginger slices and salted plums laid out on the coffee table, and then running back to Aunt Baba. All of us beckoned to her and vied for her attention as she teased us by half advancing and then quickly retreating to Aunt Baba's side.

Repeatedly, Niang signalled her baby to come to her. But, to Little Sister, her mother was a stranger and she ignored her. Niang was dressed in a dark-brown Parisian silk dress, with dangling pearl earrings and a string of large pearls around her neck. Five metres away, I could still smell the cloying, fragrant aroma of her perfume.

Trying to help, Aunt Baba unwrapped a piece of candy and waved it. Little Sister ran eagerly towards our aunt. Aunt Baba handed the candy to Niang, who waved it back and forth, attempting to entice her daughter to go to her. Rejecting the bribe and becoming annoyed, Little Sister ran to the candy dish instead and tipped its contents onto the carpet.

Growing visibly impatient, Niang approached Little Sister while we scrambled to pick up the candies. 'Bad girl!' four-year-old Fourth Brother screamed at his baby sister.

'You shouldn't have done that!' Big Sister added in a stern voice, trying to curry favour with Niang. The rest of us remained silent.

'Don't want you!' Little Sister said directly to Niang in a distinct voice. 'Don't like you. Go away!'

Surprised and hurt, Niang bent down to pick up her baby, who was wriggling and resisting with all her might. An unnatural hush fell upon the room. All eyes were on them as mother and daughter struggled. Little Sister was now howling at the top of her voice while tears rolled down her little cheeks. 'Don't want you!' she repeated loudly. 'Aunt Baba! Aunt Baba! Tell her to go away! *Go away!*'

No one said a word as Niang carried her weeping and kicking child to place her firmly on the couch next to her. Little Sister was pushing blindly against her mother's neck and face, now red and contorted with frustration. '*Keep still!*' Niang screamed futilely, again and again, in a piercing voice. In the mêlée, the string holding her pearls broke and the precious gems tumbled one by one, rolling across the carpet, onto the wooden floor.

This proved simply too much for Niang. Thoroughly exasperated, she gave a stinging slap across her baby's face. Little Sister only cried louder. Deliberately and viciously, Niang now set about beating her daughter in earnest. Her blows landed indiscriminately on Little Sister's ears, cheeks, neck and head. Everyone cowered as the punishment went on and on. The grown-ups avoided looking at each other while we children shrank into our seats.

I couldn't understand why Father, Ye Ye and Aunt Baba were making no attempt to stop the assault. Why wasn't anyone objecting? I wanted to run away but dared not move. I knew I should remain silent but words choked me and I felt compelled to spit them out. Finally I could bear it no longer. Quaking with terror, I blurted out, 'Don't beat her any more. She is only a baby!'

My protest seemed to halt Niang in the midst of her frenzy. Little Sister's screams also simmered down to a whimper. Niang glared at me. Her large, prominent eyes appeared to be popping out of their orbits with fury. 'How *dare* you!' she hissed. For a few seconds, I was fearful she was going to pounce on me instead. Across the room, Aunt Baba gave me a warning look and a slight shake of her head to say no more.

In those few moments, we had understood everything. Not only about Niang, but also about all the grown-ups. Now that Nai Nai was dead, there was no doubt who was in charge.

Fuming with rage, Niang slowly extended her right arm and pointed her index finger at me. I felt panic-stricken and saw only my stepmother's long, red, polished and perfectly manicured fingernail aimed straight at me. Then I heard her words, loaded with malice, which made my heart jump and the hair stand up on the back of my neck. 'Get out!' she snarled in a cold, distinctive voice. 'I shall never forgive you! Never! Never! Never! You'd better watch out from now on! You will *pay* for your arrogance!'

8. Tram Fare
車錢

THOUGH Father sent us to expensive missionary schools, he and Niang instituted an austerity programme to teach us the 'value of money'. To begin with, we were given no pocket-money whatsoever, not even the tram fare. We had nothing to wear except our school uniforms. Big Sister and I were ordered to keep our hair-cuts short, straight and old-fashioned. For my three brothers, it was much worse. Their heads were shaved bald in the style of Buddhist monks, and they were teased mercilessly by their peers.

My school was one and a half miles from home and situated immediately adjacent to Big Sister's. The number 8 tram ran directly from door to door. St John's Academy was three miles away and could be reached by the same number 8 tram travelling in the opposite direction.

When Ye Ye first arrived in Shanghai, we begged him for money and he gave us our tram fare to go to school. Two months later, Ye Ye had spent all his money and he brought up the subject one evening. Dinner was almost over and everyone was eating fruit when Aunt Baba mentioned that she had decided to go back to work as a bank teller at Grand Aunt's bank. (Grand Aunt was the highly successful younger sister of Ye Ye. Many years before, she had founded the Women's Bank of Shanghai and had become fabulously rich.) This was probably Aunt Baba's way of reminding Father that she and Ye Ye had run out of money for their daily needs. We were all holding our breath on their behalf.

Father and Niang looked annoyed. 'You don't need to work like a commoner,' Father said. 'You have everything you need here. Besides, Ye Ye enjoys your companionship at home. If either of you need money, why don't you come to us and ask? I've told you both before that if I'm busy or in the office, all you have to do is speak to Jeanne (Niang) here and she'll give it to you.'

How is this possible? I asked myself. Where is Ye Ye's own money? Is he no longer head of our family? Why is he suddenly and mysteriously dependent on Father and Niang for pocket-money? It made me cringe to think of my gentle and dignified grandfather begging for pocket-money from my haughty stepmother.

'You are both so generous and employ so many servants that I find little I can do to help,' Aunt Baba replied politely. 'The children are away all day at school. Going out to work every day will get me out of the house and give me something to do.'

Father now appealed to Ye Ye. 'What do you think? Won't you miss her?'

'Let her work if that's what she enjoys,' Ye Ye answered. 'She likes to spend her salary on playing mah-jong and buying treats for the children. By the way, I meant to mention this to you before. The children should be given a regular weekly allowance.'

'What for?' Father asked, turning to us. 'Hasn't everything been provided for you?'

'Well, for one thing,' replied Big Sister, speaking on behalf of all of us, 'we need the tram fare daily to go to school.'

'Tram fare?' Niang interjected sharply. 'Who told you you could ride the tram? Why can't you walk? Exercise is good for you.'

'It's so far to walk to St John's. By the time we get there, it'll be time to turn around and go home again,' Big Brother said.

'Nonsense!' Father exclaimed. 'Walking is good for growing children like you.'

'I loathe walking!' Big Brother grumbled. 'Especially first thing in the morning.'

'How dare you contradict your father!' Niang threatened. 'If he orders you to walk to school, then it's your duty to obey him. Do you hear?'

We were cowed into silence and looked towards Ye Ye, expecting him to come to our defence; but he kept his eyes on his plate and went on peeling his apple. Big Sister suddenly took the plunge. 'Ye Ye has always given us pocket-money. We're used to going to school by tram. Nobody in my class walks to school. Most of my classmates are driven there in private cars.'

Niang became enraged. 'Your father works so hard to support everyone under this roof,' she exclaimed in a loud, angry voice, shooting a quick glance at Ye Ye and Aunt Baba. 'How sneaky you all are to get money from Ye Ye without your father's knowledge! We send you to expensive schools so you'll grow up correctly. We certainly don't want you to be coddled into becoming idle layabouts. From now on, all of you are forbidden to go behind our backs to trouble Ye Ye or Aunt Baba for money. Do you hear?'

Though her remarks were addressed to us, they were obviously meant for Ye Ye and Aunt Baba as well. She paused briefly and then continued, 'We're not saying you're never to ride the tram again. We merely want you to acknowledge your errors in the past. Admit you've been wrong. Promise you'll change for the better. Come to us and apologise. Tell us from now on you will behave differently. We'll only give you the tram fare if you're truly contrite.'

The room was completely still. The only sound I heard was that of Ye Ye chomping on his apple. Surely he was going to say something to put Niang in her place! The maids hustled around with hot moist towels for us to wipe our fingers and mouths. Then Niang spoke again in a sugary tone, looking directly at Ye Ye with a smile. 'These tangerines are so juicy and sweet. Here, do have one! Let me peel it for you.'

*

At first, we were all mad! The whole tram-fare issue was obviously tied up somehow with the establishment of a new hierarchy within our family. Now that Nai Nai was dead, was Niang going to take over? We told each other we would always be loyal to Ye Ye. If necessary, we intended to walk to school forever (or at least until graduation) to show our allegiance to him.

Ten days later, I spotted Big Sister getting off the tram at the stop closest to our lane. Though she ignored me and I dared not say anything to her, she had obviously given in.

My three brothers held out week after week. St John's was so far from home! The weather turned cold and nasty. They were getting up in the dark and returning home exhausted. One after another, they gradually knuckled under.

Though Ye Ye and Aunt Baba both kept urging me to go downstairs and beg for my tram fare, I just couldn't do it. Why? I hardly knew myself. Something to do with loyalty, fair play, and a sense of obligation. I did not discuss this with anyone, not even my Aunt Baba. I simply couldn't force myself to go to Niang and admit that I (and therefore my Ye Ye) had erred in the past. Besides, it just didn't seem right to betray him, especially when I had begged for the money from him in the first place.

When the rains pelted down in sheets, and gales howled through the streets, I would grit my teeth as I set about the seemingly endless journey along Avenue Joffre. Arriving drenched at the school gates, I tried not to look at my schoolmates stepping daintily out of rickshaws, pedicabs, and chauffeur-driven cars. I knew some of them laughed at me behind my back and whispered to each other that I took my own Number 11 Private Tram to school daily, meaning that my legs carried me.

On Sunday afternoons, Niang frequently called out for my siblings to come downstairs to her bedroom (which Third Brother had nicknamed the 'Holy of Holies') and pick up their tram fares. Hearing this, I'd feel a stab of anguish because I was the only one always excluded. Big Sister sometimes came back upstairs to show off by laying her coins in a row on my bed and counting them aloud in front of me, one by one.

9. Chinese New Year
唐曆新年節

WE HAD been looking forward to Chinese New Year for weeks. Not only was it a holiday for all the school children in China, but for all the grown-ups as well. Even Father was taking off three whole days from work to celebrate. For the first time since our departure from Tianjin, a tailor had come to our house to measure everyone for new outfits. In China, new clothes were worn on New Year's Day to signal a new beginning.

On New Year's Eve, Father and Niang summoned us down to the Holy of Holies and gave us our new clothes. My three brothers were terribly disappointed to find three identical, loose-fitting

Chinese long gowns made of dark-blue wool, with traditional mandarin collars and cloth buttons. Big Sister was handed a padded silk Chinese qipao. I got a basic brown smock made of material left over from one of Big Sister's garments. Fourth Brother, however, received a stylish Western outfit with a Peter Pan collar and matching tie and belt, while Little Sister acquired a fashionable pink knitted dress bedecked with ribbons and bows.

We five stepchildren trooped back upstairs in disgust. My brothers threw their robes on their beds contemptuously. They had been looking forward to Western-style suits, shirts and ties. Nowadays, this was what their trend-setting schoolmates were wearing at St John's.

'Trash!' Big Brother declared, tossing his new garment in the air and kicking it. 'Who wants junk like this? You'd think we're still living in the Qing Dynasty! As if it's not bad enough to be called the "three Buddhist monks"! If they see us dressed in these outdated antique clothes, we might as well forget about going to school altogether!'

'The other day,' Third Brother complained bitterly, 'my desk partner asked me when I was going to start growing a pigtail and shave my brow. "Maybe you're planning to be the new Emperor Pu Yi and live in the Forbidden Palace!" he told me.'

'What gets me,' Big Sister said, 'is the blatant inequality between her children and us. I wouldn't mind if all seven of us were treated the same way. If they really believed in traditional clothes, then all seven children should be wearing them, not just the five of us.'

'Aside from the clothes,' Second Brother interrupted, 'what about our shaven heads? I don't see Fourth Brother sporting a Buddhist Monk Special! Why, the little princeling has his hair cut at the most fashionable children's hair stylist on Nanjing Lu. When he stands next to us, it's like we've stepped out of two different centuries!'

'Here Father wants to teach us the value of money,' Big Brother added, 'yet *her* children can order whatever they desire from the kitchen at any hour of the day or night. We're supposed to eat only three meals a day with congee and preserved vegetables for breakfast every morning, but I see Cook preparing bacon, eggs and toast, fresh berries and melon for *their* breakfast. Last Sunday, I went into the kitchen and told Cook I wanted a slice of bacon. The idiot won't even give me a straight answer. "I have my orders," he told me. "Bacon is reserved for the first floor." One day, I'm going to sock him in the mouth!'

'It's really getting intolerable!' Big Sister complained, lowering her voice and motioning me to close the door. I obeyed with alacrity, happy to be included. 'We should be careful though. Niang has her spies. That new tutor/nanny she's employed for her two children, that Miss Chien, she gives me the creeps. She is so slimy and obsequious, smiling and bowing all the time. Yesterday, she cornered me and invited me to have afternoon tea with Fourth Brother and Little Sister in their nursery. I never saw such a spread – finger sandwiches, toasted buns, chestnut cream cake, sausage rolls. Here we are restricted to breakfast, lunch and dinner and starving between meals, while our half-siblings are throwing their leftovers from their balcony to Jackie in the garden. It's so unfair! Anyway, Miss Chien kept quizzing me about Ye Ye, Aunt Baba, all of you and what we think of Niang. Of course I didn't reveal anything. I'm sure whatever I'd have said would have been reported straight back to our stepmother.'

'I simply *detest* that sneaky stool-pigeon Miss Chien,' Big Brother confessed. 'Day before yesterday, Father calls the three of us down to the Holy of Holies. *Big* lecture! "Miss Chien says that one of you was playing with the tap of the filtered water tank on the stairway. How many times have I told you not to drink out of that tank? It's *permanently* out of bounds to you, do you hear? If you want drinking water, you get it from the hot-water thermos flask in the kitchen. Otherwise you boys have a habit of leaving the tap turned on when there is temporarily no water. Later on, when the tap water percolates through the filter, there is a big pool of water on the stairs. Your mother has had enough of it!" So we deny that we even *touched* the tap. Does he believe us? Of course not! I told Father that I personally observed Miss Chien fiddling around with the tap early that morning. Probably nobody ever warned her about how finicky the water tank is. What's the end result? Father chooses to believe *her* and we each got two lashes from the dog whip! The liar! I *hate* her!'

'This just can't go on,' Big Sister declared. 'Let's get organised! If we unite together and protest in one voice, they won't ignore us. What about a hunger strike? That's sure to get their attention! Are you ready to join us, Fifth Younger Sister?'

I was thrilled that Big Sister was addressing me personally. 'Of course I am!' I exclaimed ardently. 'But I don't think a hunger strike will work. They'll probably be very happy that we're not eating. Five less mouths to feed, that's all. For a hunger strike to succeed, they've got to care whether we lived or died.'

'I'm for a revolution!' Second Brother exclaimed. 'Out and out war! We go to the kitchen, open the refrigerator, eat what we want and face the consequences. What can they do? The food's already in our stomachs being digested. Won't be so easy to get it back out.'

'You're always so impulsive and volatile!' Big Brother exclaimed critically. 'Just like that rash general Zhang Fei (張飛) in the Three Countries War. We've got to be more subtle and patient. Diplomacy and subterfuge are always superior to confrontation. Let's ask for a private conference with Father and point out the inequities in a calm, logical fashion.'

'It won't work!' Third Brother counselled. 'Father'll never come to the table without Niang. What about an anonymous letter written in

Chinese sent to Father through the mail? Niang doesn't read any Chinese. Big Sister could write it with brush and ink. Her handwriting is excellent and could pass for that of an adult!'

'Brilliant idea!' exclaimed Big Sister. 'Let's draft the letter now!' We hunched over the table muttering suggestions, becoming more and more excited at our escapade. Third Brother decided he might as well go to the bathroom and relieve himself while the letter was being written. He yanked open the door, stepped outside, and, to his horror, almost collided with Niang – who was standing immediately behind the portal with her ear glued against it.

Ashen-faced and petrified, he stared dumbly at our stepmother without fully closing the door while she looked down at him disdainfully. There was a deathly silence as they regarded each other. Third Brother started to tremble with terror.

Slowly, Niang raised her right index finger against her lips, warning him not to make a sound. She then waved him on with her open left hand.

In the bathroom, Third Brother locked the door carefully behind him. Recalling Niang's intimidating stare, sphinx-like immobility, and expression of distinctive menace, he was seized by a surge of nausea. How long had she been listening? What had she heard? Was everyone still plotting? Would they send him away from home? Where could he go? He vomited again and again, rinsing his mouth out over and over at the tap, dreading the moment of truth. If only he could postpone his return indefinitely and stay here forever! Alone. Uninvolved. Away from everyone. Behind a locked door . . .

A thought suddenly hit him like a blow. What if Niang was still waiting for him to go back? Could his absence be construed as a deliberate warning to the others that something was afoot? How long had he been away? He felt his mouth go dry as he quickly flushed the toilet and stumbled out. His legs seemed to keep buckling under in an extraordinary way.

He hurried back and noticed at once that no one was standing outside his bedroom door. A wave of relief washed over him. True, the door was still slightly ajar, the way he'd left it. But Niang was no longer there. He could clearly hear the murmur of Big Sister's voice, tinged with purpose and excitement, drifting down the corridor. Niang must have caught every word.

He returned and collapsed in his seat, absolutely drained. 'It's over! We're doomed!' he cried tremulously, quaking with fear. In a leaden voice, he related his encounter with Niang outside the bedroom door.

A profound and uneasy silence came over us. We stared at each other, dumbfounded. Slowly but methodically, we set about destroying all the draft copies of the incriminating 'anonymous' letter of appeal to Father. Big Sister tore the paper into shreds while muttering, 'Deny everything!' over and over. Big Brother lit a match and reduced the whole lot to ashes that we scattered outside the window. When the dinner-bell rang, we trooped downstairs stoically to face the music, telling each other we were in this together and would resist with a united front.

We were prepared for confrontation but dinner came and went without incident. In fact, Niang seemed more cordial than usual, reminding us that the next day was Chinese New Year's. We should dress in our new clothes. As a special treat, we would first be served a salted duck egg for breakfast, then Father would take us for a drive in his motor car along the Bund, the grand embankment along the river, ending with a visit to our Grand Aunt's bank at 480 Nanjing Lu, where we had all been invited to lunch.

When we returned upstairs after dinner and still nothing had been mentioned, we could hardly believe our good luck. Then we began to question Third Brother's sanity, but he stuck to his story. 'Perhaps,' he suggested darkly, 'we're being deliberately kept in a state of uncertainty because that's what Niang most enjoys. The cat-and-mouse game.' Once again, we began to feel sick with apprehension but there was nothing we could do but wait.

What Niang decided to do was to divide our loyalty towards each other by recruiting our leader, Big Sister, over to 'their' side.

The next day, as we rose from the table after a festive New Year's dinner, Niang smiled at Big Sister and invited her to move downstairs into a spare bedroom on the first floor, *their* floor.

Her offer aroused a number of disturbing emotions among us.

After Big Sister moved down to the first floor, she started assuming airs and distancing herself from those of us left on the floor above. She yearned to gain Niang's favour and gradually came to realise the importance of being on good terms with Miss Chien. The latter shared a room with Niang's two children and catered to their every wish, particularly those of Fourth Brother, Niang's favourite darling. As the days went by, Big Sister's attitude towards Miss Chien underwent a profound change. The two became friends, bound by a mutual aptitude and appetite for intrigue. Big Sister would scurry around to Niang at every opportunity to list her grievances against her former allies, fawning on those in favour and gossiping about those fallen from grace. She vaunted her newfound power to instil fear and Niang rewarded her with special favours: gifts, pocket-money, outings with friends.

There were no more private gatherings among the five of us, let alone anonymous letters to Father.

Full of envy and discontent, we four met to discuss the situation.

'Why is *she* being so favoured?' Big Brother asked. 'This has been especially noticeable since Niang eavesdropped on us on New Year's Eve. Niang must have learnt then that Big Sister is our so-called leader. She is the only one capable of disguising her handwriting to write a credible anonymous letter to Father in Chinese. What's going on between her and Niang? I don't trust either of them. They are two of a kind and will hatch up something horrible when they team up like this.'

'She has allegiance to Niang written all over her face,' Second Brother added. 'She makes me sick.'

'She probably makes up outrageous lies about us and adds oil and soya sauce to everything Niang relishes to hear,' agreed Third Brother. 'Her method of getting ahead is to inform on everyone up here.'

'The maids were moving furniture into her room yesterday. The door was open so I went in,' confided Big Brother. 'Do you know she now has her own writing desk and chest of drawers? Here the three of us have to share a room but she not only has a room to herself but a lacy white bedspread and curtains to match! While I was looking around she sneaked behind me and tapped me on the shoulder. "In future, knock and ask permission before coming in here!" she commanded. I almost threw up when I heard her aggressive and overbearing voice! You'd think she had turned into Niang herself!'

'She has obviously defected,' Third Brother related. 'The way she struts around! Yesterday I was coming up the stairs when I saw Big Sister at the doorway of Fourth Brother's bedroom, begging him for a "teeny weeny" piece of chocolate cake to tide her over until dinner. It made me ill to watch her sucking up to the wily little squirt! Grovelling and demeaning herself like that! What sort of leader is she anyway? Whose side is she on? I'd rather *starve* to death than lick the boots of Fourth Brother.'

Big Brother turned to me. 'I saw Big Sister with her arm around you yesterday asking you questions. *Beware of her!* She is an expert at feigning affection. Don't trust her or tell her anything! Otherwise you'll get hurt. Just remember, she is not like other people's big sisters! She doesn't love anyone, certainly not *you*. If she can, she will do you in!'

There was no doubt about it. In no time at all, Big Sister had completely gone over to the other side.

I grew even closer to my aunt. Our room became my refuge. Coming home from school every afternoon, I was ever so glad to cross its threshold, close the door, and spread out my books. Doing homework was the only way to cushion me from the harrowing uncertainties all around.

I knew Niang loathed me and despised my aunt. It saddened me that Aunt Baba seemed to be under a life sentence of subordination. Though I was little, I understood the awkwardness of her position: how Niang's wishes always took precedence, how she had to demonstrate caution, submission and humility at every turn.

I found it impossible to speak of this. It was simply too painful. Instead, I tried to make it up to my aunt by studying hard and getting perfect report cards. Besides, that seemed to be the only way to please my father or get any attention from him whatsoever.

I was seven years old and in the second grade. The girls in my class nicknamed me 'Genius' – partly because of my perfect scholastic record, but also because of my compositions and short stories.

I started writing by accident. Mrs Lin, my teacher in Chinese literature whose daughter Lin Tao-tao was my classmate, once gave our class a homework assignment: to write a composition titled 'My Best Friend'. Most girls wrote about their mothers. I didn't know mine so I wrote of my aunt.

My aunt and I share a room. She is my best friend and cares about me in every way. Not only about my hair, my clothes and how I look; but also about my studies, my thoughts and who I am. Though I am really nothing, she makes me believe I am special. When I get a good report card, she locks it in her safe-deposit box, and wears the key around her neck even when she sleeps, as if my grades were her most cherished treasures.

My mama and my aunt used to be best friends. Sometimes I dream of my mama on my walks to and from school. I think Mama lives high up on a mountain in a magic castle. One day, if I am really good and study very hard, she will ride down on a cloud to rescue me and take me to live with her. Nothing in Shanghai can compare with her place. It's a fairyland full of fragrant flowers, towering pines, lovely rocks, soaring bamboos and chirping birds. Every child can enter without a ticket and girls are treated the same as boys.

No one is sneered at or scolded without a reason. It's called Paradise.

Mrs Lin gave me a high mark and pinned my composition on the bulletin board. From then on, I wrote whenever I had a spare moment. It thrilled me to bring my literary efforts to school, and to see my classmates pass them illicitly from desk to desk. Groups of girls would gather around me during recess to discuss my stories, or to hear me read aloud the latest escapades of my imaginary heroines.

To me, writing was pure pleasure. It thrilled me to be able to escape the horrors of my daily life in such a simple way. When I wrote, I forgot that I was the unwanted daughter who had caused my mother's death. I could be anybody I wished to be. In my narratives, I poured out everything that I dared not say out loud in real life. I was friends with the beautiful princesses and dashing knights who lived in my imagination. I was no longer the lonely little girl bullied by her siblings. Instead I was the female warrior Mulan who would rescue her aunt and Ye Ye from harm.

In time, my stories became real to my schoolmates also. Once I used the surname Lin (林) to portray a villain. Lin Tao-tao read the tale, angrily erased Lin and scribbled Yen (嚴, my family name) in its place. A quarrel ensued between us, each enraged because the other had used her name in such a fashion. When I tried to rub out my name and re-insert hers, Lin Tao-tao suddenly burst into tears.

'It's only make-believe!' I protested, feeling ashamed for having made her cry.

'No! It isn't! You know it isn't! Look, you're rubbing so hard, you've made a hole in the paper!'

We both stared at the hole – and suddenly it struck me that we were arguing over nothing. I pointed to the hole and started to giggle. 'We're quarrelling over a hole,' I told her. 'A hole is nothing! We're fighting about nothing!'

Soon, she was laughing too. 'How about calling your villain Wu-ming (No Name 無名)?' she suggested. 'That way, nothing becomes No Name and nobody gets mad at anybody!'

'Brilliant! Let's shake hands on that!'

So the title of my story became 'The Villain with No Name'.

*

In spite of my writing and academic record, my classmates probably suspected there was something pathetic about me. I never spoke of my family; neither issued nor accepted any invitations outside the school; and always refused to eat the candies or snacks brought by my friends. My hair-style, shoes, socks and book bag did not inspire envy. No one from home ever came to be with me on prize-giving day, regardless of how many awards I had won.

They didn't know that, in front of them, I was desperate to keep up the pretence that I came from a normal, loving family. I couldn't possibly tell anyone the truth: how worthless and ugly Niang made me feel most of the time; how I was held responsible for any misfortune and was resented for simply being around; how my mind was racked with anxiety and constantly burdened by an impending sense of doom. How I simply loathed myself and wished I could disappear, especially when I was in front of my parents.

The worst of it was that I could see no way out. That was why I found it hard to fall asleep and sometimes still wet my bed in the middle of the night. But, if I tried to be really good and studied very very hard, perhaps things would become different one day, I would think to myself.

Meanwhile, I must not tell anyone how bad it really was. I must just go to school every day and carry inside this dreadful loneliness, a secret I could never share. Otherwise the guise would be over, and Father and Niang would never come to love me.

10. Shanghai School Days
上 海 小 學 生

OF ALL the girls in my class at Sheng Xin School, Wu Chun-mei was the most athletic. She came from one of Shanghai's wealthiest merchant families and lived in an imposing mansion near the French Club, which I passed daily on my way to and from school. Her father had spurned commerce for medicine and attended medical school in the United States, where Chun-mei was born. Her mother was a well-known artist and book illustrator. Being an only daughter, Chun-mei was privileged in many ways.

I first noticed Wu Chun-mei when we played shuttlecock against each other one day during recess. A shuttlecock was a rounded piece of cork with feathers stuck on top. When the shuttlecock was hit to and fro with a racket across a net, the game was called badminton. At Sheng Xin, we sometimes used the shuttlecock to play a different game. We would kick it up and down and add up the number of kicks made without interruption. The girl with the highest number was the winner.

I had always considered myself a skilful player, but my first game against Wu Chun-mei turned into an exhibition featuring my opponent's talent. Unlike the rest of us, who counted ourselves pretty lucky if we could kick the shuttlecock fifteen times in a row, Wu Chun-mei could go on indefinitely. While kicking the shuttlecock frontways, sideways and behind her, she could also clap her hands, twist her legs and even turn her body all the way around.

In due course, I became more and more impressed by Wu Chun-mei's athletic skills. She had strength, agility, co-ordination and amazing prowess at all types of physical games, especially ping-pong, badminton and volley-ball. Best of all, she possessed a single-minded fierceness, a sort of fearless loyalty towards her team-mates. Like me, she also loved to read. Unlike me, she was able to bring to school an incredible variety of children's books – many translated from foreign languages – which she generously lent to everyone.

One morning, on her way to school in her father's chauffeur-driven car, she saw me plodding along, carrying my heavy book bag. She asked her driver to stop, and offered me a lift. Though sorely tempted, I had no choice but to refuse, saying with a laugh that I enjoyed walking. Chun-mei made nothing of it until two weeks later. It had been raining very hard and the streets were flooded. There were typhoon warnings and school had been let out early. Many of the girls were stranded, waiting to be picked up by their families. Chun-mei had phoned her father, who came at once in his car to fetch her. On their way home they saw me sloshing through ankle-deep water.

Wu Chun-mei stopped the car and rolled down the window. 'Who's this lone small figure struggling along deserted Avenue Joffre braving the elements?' her father asked. 'How about a ride?'

'No, no, thank you!' I began, desperately clutching my book bag with one hand and my umbrella with the other. 'It's fun to walk in a storm like this ...' As I spoke, a gust of wind almost lifted me off the pavement. My umbrella turned inside out and I was blown sideways against a lamp-post.

Suddenly, Dr Wu got out of his car into the pouring rain, looking almost angry. 'Don't you know it's dangerous to walk in weather like this?' he asked. Then he physically bundled me into the back seat. I was drenched through and through from head to toe. The water in my shoes made a puddle on the car mat. Rivulets of water dripped from my hair, which was plastered against my head. I had no raincoat. My uniform stuck to my frame, and I was shivering. I knew I looked awful but felt I must keep up appearances. So I smiled, and spoke of the storm as if it were a great adventure. At the entrance to my lane, I insisted on getting out and walking to my house because I was terrified of getting into trouble for having accepted a lift. I simply could not run the risk of having Niang see me being driven to the front door in a car. They must have thought I was mad when I stepped back into the storm.

Wu Chun-mei and I became friends, and partnered each other when we played doubles in ping-pong or badminton. She lent me her books, and I helped her with arithmetic. Though Chun-mei excelled in English and spoke it without an accent, she was hopeless at maths, and often came under the teacher's fire.

Though her chauffeured car invariably awaited her when school finished, she often chose to walk with me until we reached her house, with her driver trailing behind at snail's pace. In the mornings, if she happened upon me trudging along, she would order her driver to stop, and would hop out and accompany me all the way.

In August 1945, when I was almost eight years old, America dropped the atom bomb on Japan. This ended the Second World War. America was the new conqueror.

At school, we were given surplus C-rations for our lunch, left by China's new heroes, the US marines. We ate hard biscuits, canned meats and chunks of bittersweet chocolate. After each meal, we prayed and thanked our American allies for winning the war.

Hollywood movies swept into Shanghai like a tidal wave. There was a craze for everything American. One day in September 1945, all the children in my school were bussed to the Bund to welcome the American soldiers. Along with my schoolmates, I cheered, waved welcoming flags, curtsied and presented bouquets. American minesweepers, cruisers and flagships clogged the muddy waters of the Huangpu River. Hotels and office buildings on the Bund were taken over by the US Navy and other American servicemen.

Photographs of American movie stars adorned billboards and magazine covers. Clark Gable, Vivien Leigh, Lana Turner and Errol Flynn became household names. One schoolmate two years ahead of us in Form 5 actually received an autographed photo from Clark Gable, sent all the way to Shanghai from Hollywood, California. She was surrounded by half the school at recess. We were borne on a frenzy of excitement at the sight of the picture of the handsome actor, each of us clamouring to hold him in our hands and gaze into his dreamy eyes – even if just for a few seconds.

About then, Wu Chun-mei lent me a book entitled *A Little Princess*, translated from English into Chinese. She told me it was one of her favourites and had been written by an English author named Frances Hodgson Burnett. This fairy-tale of seven-year-old motherless Sara Crewe, who started life as an heiress, turned overnight into a penniless servant girl and eventually changed her life through her own efforts, gripped my imagination as no other book had ever done before. I read it again and again, suffered Sara's humiliation, cried over her despair, mourned the loss of her father and savoured her final triumph. I kept it so long that Wu Chun-mei became impatient, and demanded its return. Coming from a secure and happy home, Wu Chun-mei could not grasp the impact this message of hope had upon me. For the first time, I realised adults could be wrong in their judgement of a child. If I tried hard enough to become a princess inside like Sara Crewe, perhaps I, too, might one day reverse everyone's poor opinion of me.

Reluctant to relinquish my new-found treasure, I begged to keep it for another two weeks. Laboriously and doggedly, I copied the book word for word into two exercise books during this grace period, committed parts of it to memory, and slept with it under my pillow until the manuscript became tattered.

Though Wu Chun-mei and I spent numerous school hours together, not once did I mention my family or hint at the presence of a stepmother. In many ways, I envied my friend. As much as possible, in front of her, I pretended that I had loving parents too. It was simply too painful to admit the truth because then the dream would vanish forever.

During the spring term of 1946, when I was eight years old and in the third grade, Father took Niang, Big Sister, Fourth Brother and Little Sister north to reclaim his Tianjin properties. They stayed away for three months.

It was a glorious spring and early summer. Though outwardly everything remained the same while my parents were away, in reality nothing was. The four of us left behind stepped back through time into a cheerful, buoyant and light-hearted era which we had almost forgotten.

My two oldest brothers started staying late after school to play with their friends. They refused to submit to any more head shaves, insisting on crew cuts as a compromise. They raided the refrigerator at will and ate whatever they fancied. They started taking an interest in girls, whistling after pretty ones the way the American boys did in Hollywood movies.

One Sunday morning at breakfast, Big Brother pushed aside his usual congee and preserved vegetables and told the maid his palate needed a change.

'Seeing it's Sunday, how about a nice, hard-boiled, salted duck egg?' the maid suggested.

'What does Sunday have to do with anything? I'm tired of preserved vegetables and salted duck eggs. Bring me a big omelette, made with lots of chicken eggs! Put some ham in it! That's what I feel like eating.'

'Young Master (Shao Ye 少爺)! You know that chicken eggs are not allowed. Cook has orders from above. You'll get us all in trouble.'

'If you're too cowardly to talk to Cook, I'll tackle the brute myself!' Big Brother sprang up and stomped into the kitchen. Relishing his new role as young master of the house in the absence of Father, he ordered Cook to make him the 'biggest omelette of his life' with loads of ham and plenty of scallions. A battle ensued.

'We have specific instructions from your mother that chicken eggs are intended only for those on the first floor,' announced Cook haughtily, his whole posture oozing righteous indignation. 'Besides, there are not enough eggs on hand to make such an omelette as you have in mind.'

'Not enough eggs, eh?' challenged Big Brother. 'We shall see about that!' He started a systematic search, beginning with the refrigerator and ending in the larder, retrieving every egg he could find. He then methodically broke them one by one into a giant bowl.

Meanwhile, offended by Big Brother's trespass on his domain and violation of his 'orders from above', Cook was saying frostily, 'I'll have to report this egghunt of yours. Just as I am going to mention to your parents about your "airmail letters".'

He was referring to messages sent to two pretty sisters who lived immediately behind us. Their second-floor bedroom window faced the rear window of my brothers' room, separated only by an alleyway. The boys amused themselves by wrapping scribbled notes around hard candies, then using rubber-band slings to catapult them across. The day before, an errant missile had unfortunately landed on the bald head of our neighbours' cook, who had rushed over to our house to complain loudly to his counterpart.

Chagrined but defiant, Big Brother blithely whipped up all the eggs, added ham and scallions, and made himself a king-sized sixteen-egg omelette.

'You can inform on me all you want! But first I'm going to treat myself to a decent breakfast for once, whether *they* approve or not! As for your buddy, the thump to his head will probably stimulate his conk to sprout a full head of hair again! He should thank me for doing him the favour!' With that, he sailed into the dining-room with his omelette and emptied his plate with relish.

Aunt Baba, who had been working full time as a bank teller, felt freer during this period to spend most evenings and weekends after work playing mah-jong with her friends. Ye Ye grew close to Third Brother and me, and often escorted the two of us to picnics at Du Mei Gardens, a public park one tram-stop from home.

Cook would prepare wonderful sandwiches for us, inserting thick layers of eggs flavoured with mushrooms and ham into loaves of fresh, crusty French baguettes. I used to chase Third Brother along the winding paths of the meticulously manicured arbour, hide behind giant sycamore trees, and roll across lush green lawns which spread out as far as my eyes could see. Happy and relaxed, I'd watch Third Brother imitate Ye Ye in his Tai-chi exercises; stand on tiptoe and crane my neck to catch a glimpse of famous players competing in Chinese chess; and listen to professional storytellers spinning yarns about kung-fu heroes. Sometimes, if we were lucky, a band would be playing music from the domed pavilion in the centre of the park.

We'd play for hours, pretending to be characters from Chinese folklore, taking turns as the hero or villain. When Third Brother was away from our two oldest brothers and Big Sister, he seemed to turn into a different person.

'I like you much better when I play only with you,' I confided one day. 'You don't order me around or make me be the bad person all the time when we play "Three Countries War". You are fair while the others despise me.'

'It all stems from our mama dying when you were born. Big Sister and our two older brothers knew her better than I did. I only remember her a little. Things were much nicer when she was alive. You made her go away.'

'We all live in our big house and it's full of people but it's a lonely place,' I said. 'I can't wait to grow up and get away. I'll take Ye Ye and Aunt Baba with me. You can come too if you like. It's not only Niang. Big Sister and Second Brother are always picking on me too. They *hate* it when I top my class and Father praises me. Then they're specially mean. They think I don't know but I do.'

'It's pretty bad for me too, sharing a room with our two big brothers. When things don't go well, they take it out on me. Big Brother yells at me and Second Brother beats me up and grabs my stuff.'

'How were things different when our own mama was still alive? Do you sometimes think of her too?'

'Of course! When she was with us, everything was just nicer and I remember feeling safe all the time. Wouldn't it be splendid if we could go visit her where she is now? Away from our real home where I have to be careful not to say the wrong thing.'

'But we *can* go visit her!' I said. 'All you have to do is close your eyes and imagine it. I have seen her place before. It's so real I find it hard to tell whether I saw it or dreamed it. She lives in a magic garden high up in the clouds. Nothing in Shanghai can compare. It's full of trees, flowers, rocks and birds. All children are welcome. If no one knows about her place and we keep it a secret, then they can never find us. I wrote it all down once and showed it to Big Sister. I asked her what our mama looked like, because I couldn't picture her face. Big Sister said she didn't remember.'

'*Big Sister!* How can you confide your real feelings to Big Sister! How stupid you are! If you want to know about our mama, why don't you ask Aunt Baba? As for Big Sister, don't trust her! Don't trust anyone! *Be a cold fish, just like me.* Never get involved. That's my motto. I hurt no one. And no one can hurt me.'

I thought over his advice. That evening, I broached the subject with my aunt. 'Tell me what my real mama looked like. I have this key in my head which enables me to enter the secret kingdom where she lives, but I would like to see her photograph. I can't picture her face.'

'Your father has instructed me not to talk to you children about your dead mother ...' It seemed hard for Aunt Baba to utter the words 'your dead mother'. 'But I suppose you're old enough now to understand, there *are* no photographs of her. Shortly after your grandmother's funeral three years ago, your father ordered all her photographs destroyed.'

One week later, Shanghai was gripped by a relentless, blistering heatwave. Finally, Sunday came and there was no school. Ye Ye and Aunt

Baba had gone to the Buddhist Temple. It was early afternoon and a heavy drowsiness shrouded the entire house. I had just completed my homework and was rereading my latest report card while relaxing on my bed under the mosquito net. Though the windows were wide open, there was no breeze.

I was recalling the excitement in my classroom two days before, when the half-term exam marks were read out. My classmates sat in rapt attention as Teacher Lin rustled some papers and looked for her glasses. I relived the triumph of hearing Teacher Lin announce, 'Yen Jun-ling* has topped the class again in every subject except art. I commend her for her hard work. Earlier this year the school submitted one of her compositions to the Children's Writing Competition held by the Shanghai Newspaper Association. I am glad to report that she has won first prize for her age group among all the primary school students in Shanghai. Yen Jun-ling has brought recognition to our Sacred Heart School.'

Amidst loud clapping and the admiration of my peers, I stepped forward to shake hands with

* My name as used outside the family.

Teacher Lin. She handed me a special gold star to paste on my report card, as well as a copy of the newspaper in which my composition had been published.

To everyone's surprise and my delight, my ping-pong partner Wu Chun-mei received two special prizes: a medal for being the outstanding athlete of the whole school and a certificate for showing the most improvement in arithmetic. Wu Chun-mei blushed with pleasure when Teacher Lin pinned the medal on her uniform. I whispered 'champion' and patted her on the back when she returned to her seat.

How wonderful life is at this moment! I thought as I fanned myself and wriggled my toes. With Father and Niang gone, the whole house seemed relaxed and carefree. If only it weren't so hot!

I was scanning the other children's winning entries in the newspaper when the maid came in and announced, 'Your brothers want you to go downstairs and play with them in the dining-room. They have a treat for you!'

I was dizzy with excitement as I crawled out from under my mosquito net and slipped on my shoes. 'Are all three of my brothers playing in the dining-room? Is Third Brother down there too?'

'Yes, they're all there.'

How mysterious and delightful! My three big brothers beckoning me to join them! I ran downstairs eagerly, taking the steps two at a time, then sliding down the banister from the first floor to the ground floor. I burst in panting for breath.

They had been drinking orange juice and put their glasses down when I entered. On the large, oval dining-table was a large jug of juice and four glasses. Three were empty and one was full.

'What a hot day!' Second Brother began, bubbling with laughter. 'I see you're sweating! We thought you'd like a glass of juice to cool you down. Here, this one's for you!'

Something in his manner caused me to hesitate. To be summoned by Second Brother out of the blue and be treated so royally was cause for suspicion. 'Why are you so nice to me all of a sudden?' I asked.

At this he took offence. Moving closer he jostled me. 'It's because you are again top of your class. In addition, you won that writing competition held by the Shanghai Newspaper

Association. Seeing Father isn't here, we decided to reward you ourselves.'

'I don't want it!' I cried as I pushed the glass away.

'We even put ice in it so you'll cool down at once.' He picked up the glass and the ice-cubes tinkled. A film of moisture had condensed on the glass's cool surface.

Tempted, I turned to Big Brother. 'Did you make it specially for me?'

'We mixed it from this bottle of orange concentrate here. This is your prize for topping your class. Custom-made just for you!' My three brothers could hardly contain themselves with suppressed merriment.

I could feel the humid, oppressive heat seeping through the walls. I eyed the cool glass of juice with its ice-cubes rapidly melting in a shaft of sunlight slanting across the table. I lifted the glass and turned to Third Brother, my ally, knowing that *he* would never fail me. 'Can I drink this?' I asked, confident he could be relied upon.

'Of course! Congratulations! We're proud of you!'

Convinced, I took a generous sip of the ice-cold drink. The disgusting smell of urine hit me like a mighty blow. My brothers had mixed their urine with the juice. Through the mirror hanging on the wall, I could see them rolling on the floor with hysterical laughter.

I ran upstairs to the bathroom to wash out my mouth, knowing I had been duped. Sweat poured down my face and mingled with my tears as I sobbed quietly into the sink. In the suffocating heat, I was shivering.

Meanwhile, my brothers had already forgotten all about me. I could hear them in the garden playing with Jackie and kicking a ball against the wall. Pong! Pong! Pong! Woof! Woof! The raucous sound of their laughter came drifting up through the window.

Why was I crying? Surely, I was inured by now to their malice. What was it that really bothered me? Their treachery and betrayal of my trust? No, not quite, it was more complicated. Did Third Brother truly understand what he was up against? By wanting to have things both ways and straddling the fence, was he aware that each compromise would chip away at his integrity? Yes! It was the loss of the nicest parts of Third Brother which saddened me.

*

Next morning, on my way to school, Wu Chun-mei came out of her garden as soon as she saw me. She challenged me to a numbers game played with our fingers as we walked along, trailed as usual by her chauffeured car.

At a red light, an American jeep stopped beside us. Two tall blond US sailors in smart, white, sharply creased uniforms shouted out in English, 'Little girls, do you know how to get to Avenue Joffre?'

I said nothing because my English was poor and I was shy. But Wu Chun-mei answered in her best American English, 'Actually, you're on Avenue Joffre. It's a very long street which goes on and on.'

They were delighted and astonished. 'Gee, thanks!' One of them said, 'Here, you two, take this!' And he handed Wu Chun-mei a large basket of luscious red persimmons.

During recess, we examined our windfall and shared the fruits among our friends. Though my classmates often brought snacks, I never dared accept because I knew I could never reciprocate in kind. This time, however, things were different. Half the fruit had been given to me.

Though bright red and perfectly formed, the persimmons felt hard and unripe. 'Maybe we should keep them in our desks and let them ripen before we eat them,' I advised. 'Raw persimmons are so puckery on the tongue . . .'

'You're too cautious!' Wu Chun-mei said. 'There are two types of persimmons. The Fuyu persimmon is supposed to be eaten when it's like this. They're crispy and sweet, just like apples.'

'All right!' Lin Tao-tao said. 'You take a bite first, Wu Chun-mei!'

Wu Chun-mei took a big bite. 'Delicious!' she exclaimed. 'Just as I thought!'

Reassured, we each bit into our fruit – only to pucker up in total disgust. But Wu Chun-mei looked so impish and mischievous that we soon all burst out laughing.

During English class later that afternoon, we had a special visitor. An impressive-looking middle-aged American officer came in uniform to give us a talk on Pearl Harbor. He was a chain-smoker and our whole class was fascinated as we watched him. While his sentences were being translated by our English teacher, he would take a deep drag on his cigarette and, after an interval, let the smoke slowly escape from his nostrils.

At the end of his speech, we clapped politely. He then asked if there were any questions. There was a pause.

'Surely,' he coaxed, 'one of you young ladies must be curious about something!' He took another drag on his cigarette. We stared at the tendrils of smoke coming out of his nose.

Finally, after another embarrassing lull, Wu Chun-mei raised her hand.

'Now, here is a brave young girl!' he exclaimed. 'What is your question, my dear?'

'I hope you don't mind,' Wu Chun-mei asked in her flawless English. 'But can you make the smoke come out of your ears too?'

11. PLT

小 寶 貝

NOT LONG after Father and Niang returned from Tianjin, Mr and Mrs Huang came to visit. They brought gifts for all seven of us children in a large cardboard box with several holes punched in the lid. Before her marriage, Mrs Huang had worked for a few years at Grand Aunt's bank, sharing a booth with Aunt Baba and our real mama. The Huangs therefore knew of Father's first marriage and the existence of all seven children.

This was highly unusual. Most of Niang's friends were unaware that she had five stepchildren. Being only eleven years older than Big Sister, Niang was reluctant to admit she was a stepmother. When asked, she often gave the impression that Father had only two children – Fourth Brother and Little Sister.

When we opened the gift box from the Huangs, we were delighted to find seven little baby ducklings. As usual, Fourth Brother picked first, followed by Little Sister, Big Sister, Big Brother, Second Brother and Third Brother. By the time my turn arrived, I was left with the tiniest, scrawniest baby bird. I picked her up, cupped her in my hand and carried her gingerly into my room. The little duckling cocked her head to one side and looked at me with dark dewy round eyes. She waddled unsteadily and pecked the floor, looking for worms and seeds. She seemed so helpless with her soft yellow feathers, slender twiggy legs and small webbed feet. One gust of wind and she would be blown away. I felt very protective.

From that moment, I took the duckling to my heart. For the first time, I had a pet of my very own. At school, I proudly described my duckling to my classmates. As I spoke, I felt a warm, tender glow spreading all through me. I named my duckling Precious Little Treasure (Xiao Bao-bei (小 寶 貝). Wu Chun-mei advised me to call it PLT for short. I couldn't wait to rush home from school, carry PLT to my room, bathe and feed her, and do my homework with PLT wandering between the beds and my desk. It comforted me to know I was needed.

I told Wu Chun-mei, 'When I pick PLT up from her pen on the roof terrace, she cocks her head to one side and chirps as if she recognises me. As soon as she sees me, she hurries over. I speak to her all the time and I think she's beginning to understand. Can ducklings learn to quack in the Shanghai dialect? Would that sound different from Mandarin quacks or English quacks?'

Wu Chun-mei laughed. 'I believe animals do understand us,' she replied. 'Perhaps not exactly your words but a special language not made of words. Maybe it's the way you stand or how you hold her. She knows she belongs to you and you'll look after her.'

As time went on, the friendship between PLT and me deepened. When Aunt Baba came home from the bank one Friday, she overheard me talking. 'Here are two worms I dug up from the garden! Risked my life and limb for you, my friend! Jackie barked at me but I didn't stop. You'd better eat it all!'

Aunt Baba was both startled and amused. 'I just heard you speaking to PLT as if she were your baby sister, in a tone both proud and loving. Do you think PLT understands what you're saying?' she asked.

I nodded solemnly. 'She likes me to talk to her and feed her worms. She knows I dug them up specially for her. When she hears Jackie barking, she scampers away from the window as if she is afraid. When I get involved with homework and ignore her, she comes over to see what I'm doing. She knows a lot! See, she is gazing at me now, wanting to find out what we're talking about. She is a very curious bird indeed!'

I crouched down and faced my pet. PLT's body twittered and she chirped as if she were chatting to a playmate. She looked up and two round dark eyes gazed out at me from her small, yellow head. 'Look! Look! Aunt Baba! She has eaten the worms! She lets me come so close! Do you think she likes me too? She senses she is safe and I'll never frighten her. She's all mine. Tomorrow is Saturday and I can dig for worms all afternoon. Hooray!'

It was a glorious Saturday afternoon when I set foot in the garden. A faint cool breeze was blowing in from the river, sweeping away the mist and clouds. Magnolia blossoms were in full bloom, dotting the tree like giant white ribbon-bows fringed by dark-green leaves, scenting the air with a fresh, delightful fragrance. Never had the sky looked so blue.

I squatted in the corner farthest from Jackie's doghouse and dug away with an old iron spoon which Cook had discarded, wishing I had a spade. I kept one wary eye on Jackie, who was lying half in and half out of his dog-house, watching me. His mouth was open and he was panting with his large tongue hanging out between two rows of giant, sharp teeth. Just as I knew PLT was my friend, I was equally certain Jackie was not. He would probably attack me if I rubbed him the wrong way. I glanced at the large, wolf-like dog and shivered involuntarily.

Soon I came upon a worm. I freed it from the clumps of weeds, wet leaves and mud and placed it in a paper bag. PLT would be pleased. Everything smelt sweet, fresh and damp. Jackie had not stirred. His eyes were half closed, and he was breathing regularly, about to fall asleep. I tiptoed away so as not to wake him and ran upstairs directly to the duck pen on the roof terrace.

All seven ducklings scampered around to greet me joyously. Though the maids were supposed to feed them and sweep out the pen, they didn't relish the task and often neglected it. I noticed the food bowl and water pan were both empty. Since I was eager to give PLT her treat, I decided to alert the maids later.

I knelt and placed my worm in the food bowl. The entire flock crowded around, jockeying for position. Though they looked identical to the grown-ups, each was distinct and unique to us children. I was pleased to note that PLT had grown quite big and strong and was holding her own against the rest. The ducklings of Little Sister and Second Brother were aggressively jostling PLT. I tried gently to shoo them away so PLT could eat her worm in peace. I felt quite guilty about my favouritism and couldn't help blaming myself for not having procured more worms so each duckling could have its own.

Suddenly, I felt a painful blow against the back of my head. It was so hard I was knocked sideways to the ground. The ducklings scurried off in fright. I looked up to see Second Brother scowling down, arms akimbo. Apparently, he had been watching me stealthily from the landing for some time. 'This will teach you to favour *your* duck over *mine*!' he shouted. He hit me again, picked up the food bowl and ordered me to '*get lost!*' as he fed my worm to his own duckling.

I got up and turned to go. It was then that I noticed PLT. Unlike the rest, my pet had not run away but was standing faithfully by my side. Despite the pain and commotion caused by my brother's blows I found immense consolation in the knowledge that PLT was staying right by me. I picked up my bird lovingly and for a moment seemed to see my grief reflected in her round dark eyes.

Back in my room I busied myself getting some grains of rice and water for PLT. It was still early and Aunt Baba hadn't come home from the bank. PLT waddled about, busily pecking the floor, now and then coming over to look at me. 'Apart from Aunt Baba, you're the only one who's always here for me; the only one who understands. Are you reminding me that I promised you a tasty worm yesterday?' I asked in the coaxing tone I reserved for my pet. PLT looked back wistfully with her round eyes, which resembled two black gum-drops. I felt sure she understood every word. 'I bet you wish you could talk and tell me all sorts of things,' I said to my pet. 'Though Second Brother robbed you of your worm, it's not the end of the world. I'll just have to go downstairs and get you another. Wait here!'

I returned to the garden. Jackie was now wide awake and pacing the ground aggressively. Back and forth. Back and forth. He had awakened from his nap in a bad mood and was growling at me. With his long, pointed ears, triangular eyes, prominent jaws and sharp teeth, he resembled a ferocious wolf more than ever. I was quite fearful as I started to dig up a patch of earth at the foot of the magnolia tree.

Jackie fidgeted, pawed the ground, and started to bark at me. I could see the tail end of a worm burrowing rapidly beneath a clump of roots. Though I knew I had incurred Jackie's displeasure in some way, I was reluctant to leave empty-handed. Keeping one eye on the worm, I half turned towards Jackie, who was baring his teeth in a most menacing manner. Tentatively, I stretched out my left hand to calm him while clutching the spoon in my right. Suddenly, Jackie lunged at me and sank his teeth into my outstretched left wrist.

Abandoning my spoon, I hurried away. PLT greeted me expectantly at the door but I rushed past into the bathroom to wash away the blood trickling down my left arm. Footsteps sounded from the landing. Aunt Baba had finally come home from the bank.

'What happened to you?' she asked in alarm, and something in her voice made the tears well up in my eyes. Baba hurried over and held out her arms, rocked me back and forth, dried my tears and asked, 'Are you hurt? Is it bad?' She wiped away the blood, washed my wrist, dressed the wound with mercurochrome, cotton-wool and a small bandage. She then walked over and locked our bedroom door, followed and watched by PLT every step of the way. She seated me on my bed and smoothed my hair. 'It's better not to mention any of this at dinner tonight unless you are asked directly,' she advised. 'Jackie is *their* pet. Don't make any waves. I tell you what. Let's open my safe-deposit box and take a look. That'll make us both feel much better.'

Aunt Baba rummaged through a pile of folded towels in her cupboard, underneath which she had hidden her safe-deposit box. She unlocked it with the key on the gold chain she wore around her neck. This was where she kept her scanty collection of precious jewels, some American dollar bills, a sheaf of yellowed letters, and all my report cards, from kindergarten to the most recent.

We gazed first at those reports written in French from St Joseph's kindergarten in Tianjin; then the ones for the first and second grades written in Chinese from Sheng Xin Primary School in Shanghai. Even PLT stopped her wandering to sit contentedly at our feet, looking up occasionally as if wishing to participate.

'See this one?' Aunt Baba exclaimed with pride. 'Six years old, all of first grade and already top in Chinese, English and arithmetic. At this rate nobody going to university can have a better foundation. When you get to be twelve you should sit for the examination to enter McTyeire where your Grand Aunt went. Then go on to university. You can be anything you set your mind to be. Why, you might even become the president of your own bank one day!'

'Will you come and live with me if I'm president?' I asked wistfully. 'I wouldn't want to own a bank without you.'

'Of course I will! We'll set up house on our own and take PLT with us. We'll work together in our own bank, side by side. Mark my words, if you study hard, anything is possible!'

'I will study hard! I promise!'

The truth was that as soon as I heard Aunt Baba's footsteps, I started feeling better immediately. Knowing there was someone who cared for and believed in me had revived my spirit. So we chattered happily about this and that until dinner-time.

The breeze died down and it became very warm as the evening meal progressed. As usual, all the dishes were served at once: cold cucumber chunks marinated in vinegar and sugar; tofu with minced pork and chopped peanuts; sautéed shrimp with fresh green peas; steamed stuffed winter melon; sweet-and-sour pork with pineapple slices; stewed duck with leeks. After the grown-ups were served, we children were each handed a bowl of steamed rice and an assortment of the day's dishes. We were expected to consume every morsel of food on our plates. It was frowned upon to leave any scraps behind, even one grain of rice.

Ever since the arrival of PLT, I had started to hate eating duck in any form or shape. It seemed wrong to eat an animal of the same species as my darling pet. Aside from duck, Third Brother and I shared an aversion to fatty meat, taking great pains to hide or discard any fat on our plates. I

Grand Aunt She was also known as Grand Uncle: Gong Gong because of the respect granted her as president of the Shanghai Women's Bank, which she founded in 1924.

The seven of us with Jackie This picture was taken in 1946, about the time that we were given a little duckling as a pet. I was eight years old.

Niang, Ye Ye and Father Ye Ye was a devout Buddhist. He always shaved his head, wore a skullcap in winter, and dressed in Chinese robes.

Aunt Baba This photograph was taken in the 1930s. Aunt Baba never married and was financially dependent on my father and stepmother all her life. I loved her very much.

now looked with revulsion at my portion of duck meat with its underlying layer of soft yellow fat. Apparently Third Brother felt the same because I saw him extract his piece of duck when no one was looking and slip it into his trouser pocket.

I had eaten everything except my duck. Slowly, I lifted the duck with my chopsticks and let it drop to the table as if by accident. Father was complaining of the heat. I watched the beads of sweat glistening on his forehead and wondered why he didn't remove his jacket and tie. Every night he and Niang came down to dinner dressed to the nines: he in a stiff white shirt, knotted black tie, long pants and matching jacket; she in a stylish dress with all her make-up and not a hair out of place. Wouldn't he be more comfortable in a tennis shirt and shorts and she in a loose house dress?

I was thinking of sticking the piece of duck to the bottom of the dining-table when I saw Niang glancing at me suspiciously. Quickly, I popped the revolting morsel into my mouth and held it there without chewing or swallowing. Niang was instructing the maid to bring in a fan.

Muttering about having to go to the bathroom, I rushed out, spat my mouthful into the toilet and flushed it down.

When I returned, Niang was describing the dog-obedience lesson she had received with Jackie from Hans Herzog that morning. Mr Herzog was a renowned German dog-trainer. His lessons were highly selective because Jackie was being taught to obey only Father, Niang and Fourth Brother, who took turns attending Mr Herzog's sessions with Jackie.

'Is Jackie making any progress?' Father asked.

'It's hard to judge because I see Jackie every day,' Niang answered. 'I certainly *hope* Jackie is learning something because Mr Herzog has raised his fees again! My driving lessons are now cheaper than Jackie's obedience lessons.'

'Since it's so hot tonight,' Father suggested, 'why don't we all cool off in the garden after dinner? It will also give us a chance to test Jackie's obedience.' He turned to Big Brother. 'Go fetch one of those ducklings that the Huangs brought. We'll have some fun tonight!'

There was a momentary silence. To us children, Father's announcement was like a death sentence. Immediately, I had a picture in my mind of my pet being torn to pieces between Jackie's frothing, ravenous jaws. I felt as if my heart had stopped beating. I held myself rigid, in a world full of dread, knowing with absolute certainty that the doomed duckling would be mine.

Big Brother scraped back his chair, ran upstairs and came down with PLT. Everyone avoided looking at me. Even Aunt Baba could not bear to meet my eyes. Father strode into the garden with PLT on his palm and sat down on a lounge chair, flanked by all the grown-ups. We children sprawled in a semi-circle on the grass. Jackie greeted his master joyfully, wagging his tail and jumping up and down with happiness.

Father released PLT and placed her in the centre of the lawn. My little pet appeared bewildered by all the commotion. She stood quite still for a few moments, trying to get her bearings: a small, yellow, defenceless creature beset with perils, surrounded by humans wanting to test their dog in a gamble with her life. I sat stiffly with downcast eyes. For a moment, I was unable to focus properly. Don't move, PLT! Please don't move! I prayed silently. As long as you keep still, you have a chance!

Jackie was ordered to 'sit' about two metres away. He sat on his hind legs with his large tongue hanging out, panting away. His fierce eyes were riveted on his prey. Father kept two fingers on his collar while the German Shepherd fidgeted and strained restlessly.

The tension seemed palpable while I hoped against hope that fate could be side-stepped in some way. Then PLT cocked her head in that achingly familiar way of hers and spotted me. Chirping happily, she waddled unsteadily towards me. Tempted beyond endurance, Jackie sprang forward. In one powerful leap, he broke away from Father's restraint and pounced on PLT, who looked up at me pleadingly, as if I was supposed to have an answer to all her terror.

Father dashed over, enraged by Jackie's defiance. Immediately, Jackie released the bird from his jaws, but with a pang I saw PLT's left leg dangling lifelessly and her tiny, webbed foot twisted at a grotesque angle. Blood spurted briskly from an open wound.

I was overwhelmed with horror. My whole world turned desolate. I ran over without a word, cradled PLT tenderly in my arms and carried her upstairs. Placing her on my bed, I wrapped my mortally wounded pet in my best school scarf and lay down next to her. It was a night of grief I have never forgotten.

I lay there with my eyes closed pretending to be asleep but was actually hopelessly awake. Surely everything would remain the same as long as I kept my eyes shut and did not look at PLT. Perhaps, when I finally opened them again after wishing very hard all night, PLT's leg would miraculously be healed.

Though it was the height of summer and Aunt Baba had lowered the mosquito net over my bed, I was deathly cold; thinking over and over, 'When tomorrow comes, will PLT be all right?'

In spite of everything, I must have dozed off because at the break of dawn, I woke up with a jerk. Beside me, PLT was now completely still. The horrors of the previous evening flooded back and everything was as bad as before. Worse, because PLT was now irrevocably dead. Gone forever.

Almost immediately, I heard Father calling Jackie in the garden. He was preparing to take his dog for their customary Sunday morning walk. At the sound of Jackie's bark, Aunt Baba suddenly sat up in her bed. 'Quick! Take this opportunity while Jackie's away! Run down and bury your pet in the garden. Get the big spade from the tool shed at the back and dig a proper hole.' She handed me an old sewing box, placed PLT's little body inside and closed the lid.

I dashed out of my room and almost collided with Big Brother, who had just come out of the bathroom in the hall.

'Where are *you* going?' he asked, full of curiosity. 'And what's that you're carrying?'

'I'm going to the garden to bury PLT.'

'Bury her! Why don't you give her to Cook and ask him to stew her for breakfast instead? Stewed duck in the evening and stewed duck in the morning! I love the taste of duck, don't you?' He saw the look on my face and knew he had gone too far. 'Look, that was a joke. I didn't really mean it. I'm sorry about last night too. I didn't know which duckling to pick when Father gave me that order. I only took yours because you're the one least likely to give me trouble afterwards. It wasn't anything against you personally, understand?'

'She was my best friend in the whole world . . .' I began, tears welling up in spite of myself. 'And now I've lost her forever.'

Halfway down the stairs, I heard Third Brother calling me from the landing. 'I've been waiting to go to the bathroom but I'll be down in the garden as soon as I can. Don't start without me.'

The two of us stood side by side, dug a hole and buried PLT under the magnolia tree with all its flowers in bloom. After that day, I was never able to smell the fragrance of magnolia blossoms again without the same aching sense of loss. We placed some grains of rice, a few worms and a little water in a shallow dish along with a bouquet of flowers in a milk bottle by PLT's grave. We bowed three times to show our respect. I cried throughout the ceremony.

Third Brother tried to comfort me. 'It won't be like this forever. *Suan le!* (算了) Let it be! Things are bound to get better. You'll see. Sometimes I can't wait to grow up so I can find out what we'll all become in twenty years' time.'

'Thanks for attending PLT's funeral so early in the morning,' I murmured as I looked down at the bandage on my left wrist. So much had happened since Jackie bit me yesterday. 'It's Sunday and everyone in the house is still sleeping. I don't know why, but I feel as if it's the two of us against the world. Whatever happens, we must never let them win.'

12. Big Sister's Wedding
大 姐 婚 禮

FATHER and Niang continued to travel to Tianjin on business. Sometimes they took Big Sister out of school to accompany them. Everyone wondered why. Did Father need Big Sister's translation skills? It soon turned out Niang had other ideas.

During the Chinese New Year holidays in 1948, Niang's plans came to light. On Sunday afternoon, Big Sister came into my room after lunch. Aunt Baba, Ye Ye and I were playing cards. She sat down on Aunt Baba's bed and told us that Father and Niang were lunching at the posh Cathay Hotel with guests from Tianjin. Dr Sung was Nai Nai's doctor and used to live next door to us. His son, Samuel, had recently returned from America and was looking for a job. Big Sister wouldn't play with us but kept doodling Chinese and English words on a sheet of paper. I leaned over and saw that she had scribbled Mrs Samuel Sung (in English and Chinese) over and over about thirty times. Then she told us Father and Niang had introduced Samuel to her, and she had agreed to marry him. She was smiling as she related this and appeared quite pleased, but I felt sad and frightened for her.

I thought to myself, Big Sister is only seventeen years old and Samuel is already thirty-one, almost twice her age. When I get to be seventeen, I sure don't want to be taken out of school to marry someone I've just met! Especially when he is so much older!

How can Big Sister remain so cheerful when her life is about to take such a ghastly turn? To be taken out of school and thrust into the arms of a stranger! No more classes! No more schoolmates! No possibility of ever going to college! Not even a high-school diploma! How devastating! What did Niang say to induce Big Sister to agree to such a fate? Why is she going along with it?

Is this going to happen to me too? I'll simply have to run away from home if Niang ever threatens to force me into an arranged marriage. But where can I go? Who will take me in? There must be millions of unwanted Chinese girls like me in Shanghai!

I imagined Niang introducing me to a strange man and ordering me to marry him. The thought filled me with horror and fear.

Weeks before Big Sister's wedding, gifts started arriving at our house. Niang carefully sorted them out and kept the best ones for herself.

Three days before the wedding, Grand Aunt personally entrusted a special small package wrapped in gold foil for Aunt Baba to hand to Big Sister. On opening the elegant leather case in Aunt Baba's room, Big Sister found a lovely pendant made of antique imperial green jade hanging from a heavy gold chain. She immediately put it on and gasped with pleasure while she admired herself in the mirror. Then she begged Aunt Baba and me not to mention Grand Aunt's gift to a soul, obviously intending to keep the pendant without telling Niang.

The wedding was a formal and brilliant affair with a banquet for five hundred in the grand ballroom on the ninth floor of the Cathay Hotel, situated at the junction of the Bund and fashionable Nanjing Lu and overlooking the Huangpu River. The room was filled with masses of fresh flowers, and the Chinese character for double happiness was outlined in red blooms against the wall. Big Sister was elegantly dressed in a beautiful pink qipao and silver shoes while Samuel wore a tuxedo. Two professional radio comedians acted as masters of ceremonies.

I had nothing to wear but an old pink qipao that had been handed down by Big Sister when she grew out of it. Though I didn't look particularly nice, at least I didn't stand out and no one noticed me. My three older brothers, however, were having a horrible time. For this special occasion, Father ordered them to have fresh hair-cuts. My brothers' heads were shaved cleanly so not a trace of hair remained. They were wearing identical, dark-blue, traditional, long Chinese robes with high collars and cloth buttons. As soon as they stepped into the foyer, I saw some boys their age pointing at them and snickering behind their backs. When they entered the main ballroom, one of the boy-guests who recognised them from St John's immediately called out to another across the room. 'Hey! It's kind of dark in here. Thank goodness three light bulbs have just walked in. With them around, there's no need for lamps.'

'Naw! Those aren't light bulbs! They are enlightened, that's all! Those are three new monks who have seen the light! They've taken the vow of chastity and abstinence. From now on, they'll eat tofu only.'

Everyone doubled up with laughter. I cringed on behalf of my brothers.

Their dilemma was compounded because all the other guests were so fashionably dressed. Men and boys wore dark, Western suits. Women were bejewelled and in silk qipaos or formal Western gowns. Fourth Brother had his hair cut in the latest page-boy manner. He looked very smart in a brand-new navy jacket with sharply creased matching trousers, white shirt and neck tie. Little Sister wore a frilly red-satin dress with ribbons in her hair and jade bracelets on her wrists.

Towards the end of the banquet, I went to the toilets. While I was inside one of the cubicles, I heard one woman remark to another about the different treatment received by Father's two sets of children from his two wives. Immediately afterwards, two other women entered. They were chatting and laughing and I recognised Grand Aunt's distinct Ningpo accent. I was about to emerge and greet her when I heard the other woman answer. It was Niang.

A chill went down my spine. I felt guilty though I had done nothing. I kept as still as a mouse and dared not move. The longer I stayed, the more impossible it became to come out.

Grand Aunt was complimenting Niang on her jade ring, telling her it had the same translucency as the jade pendant she had asked Aunt Baba to hand to Big Sister as a wedding present. In a few sentences, Niang had already found out everything without revealing she had been kept in the dark about the gift. Hearing this, I was more nervous than ever and stayed motionless in my stall until long after they had left.

I knew my sister would get into big trouble if I didn't warn her, so I waited until I saw her going by herself into her dressing-room, which was a storeroom emptied out and set aside for her to change her clothes. I told her of the conversation I had overheard between Grand Aunt and Niang.

Tears came to her eyes and she patted me fondly on my head. 'I'll never forget this kindness on your part. Thanks for the tip-off. You're the best sister in the world and I'll always be indebted to you.'

For the first time she was kind to me and I felt very close to her. Later, I saw Big Sister and Niang walking towards the balcony and talking privately just before she and Samuel left for their honeymoon. Was she able to explain it all away? I hoped so. I only wished I could have helped her more.

Next morning, Third Brother told me he was playing hide-and-seek on the balcony of the Cathay Hotel after the wedding banquet when he overheard Big Sister and Niang talking. He was hiding behind a large potted plant and could hear them very plainly.

In a tone full of regret and self-reproach, Big Sister was confessing about 'something on her conscience' which did not permit her to remain silent any longer. Although Aunt Baba had sworn her to secrecy and advised her not to reveal to Niang Grand Aunt's wedding gift of a jade pendant, she had decided to ignore Baba's instruction because our aunt was being selfish and dishonest. Besides, the piece of jade would be a perfect match for Niang's favourite jade ring and she begged Niang to accept it. In one stroke, Big Sister had endeared herself to Niang while simultaneously denouncing Aunt Baba.

Touched by Big Sister's honesty and generosity, Niang immediately allowed her to keep the jade pendant. Promising to be forever loyal to Niang regardless of Baba's sedition, Big Sister swore Niang to secrecy, thus remaining in the good graces of both while driving the wedge ever deeper between Niang and Aunt Baba. She then left on her honeymoon in an excellent mood, wearing her beautiful jade with a clear conscience.

13. A Birthday Party
生 日 慶 祝 會

A S SOON as we went back to school after the summer holidays in September 1948, Wu Chun-mei began begging me to go to her house to celebrate her birthday.

'Remember the duckling you used to have a long time ago which we nicknamed PLT?' she reminded me. 'Whatever happened to it?'

'She died,' I said rather brusquely. PLT's tragic fate was a secret locked in my heart, together with all the other unspeakable stuff I hated to think about. It was certainly not something I wished to share, let alone with someone as nice as Wu Chun-mei. She would never be able to understand. I thought of Big Sister's jade pendant and her lies about Aunt Baba, and longed to disclose to my friend all that was buried within. What if I were to suddenly blurt out, 'Should my stepmother force me into an arranged marriage like my sister's and I run away from home, will you take me in?' Would she be shocked?

Meanwhile Wu Chun-mei was saying, 'No wonder you don't speak of PLT any more. Well, for my birthday, my parents said they'd give me a pet of my very own if I promised to take care of it. They took me to the pet shop last week and I saw the most adorable puppy –'

'For me, no other pet can ever replace PLT . . .' I interrupted rudely because, for a moment, I thought I was going to cry. 'Besides,' I continued with a shrug as if I had not a care in the world, 'I'm scared of dogs. They bite!'

'This one won't! It's a little pug with big eyes and a tail which stands up. Oh, do come and see it! Mama says you can come any time that's convenient to you. It doesn't have to be on the day of my birthday. Just give her a few days' notice. You've never been to my house before and I have so many dolls and books to show you. Please say you'll come!'

I couldn't very well tell her I was forbidden to visit any of my friends, ever. For a whole week, I kept making all sorts of excuses but she was persistent. It became increasingly difficult because, inside, I was simply dying to go.

Suddenly, Teacher Wong informed us that next Tuesday would be a special school holiday because it was the name day of our new Mother Superior. She said we were lucky because all the other school children in Shanghai would still have to go to school that day. At first I was disappointed because I'd much rather go to school than stay home. Then Wu Chun-mei asked me again at recess to go play at her house. On a whim I said, 'How about next Tuesday? Instead of going to school, I'll go to your house and celebrate your birthday!'

As soon as I said this, I felt scared and wanted to back out; but Wu Chun-mei was already jumping up and down with glee. The next day, it became even more impossible to change my mind, because her birthday party had grown to include six other girls. 'They're all coming because you said you'd be there,' Wu Chun-mei exclaimed. 'It's going to be a very special occasion starting from 8.30 and ending at 3.30. My mama says she'll get out of the house so we can play in the living-room by ourselves! I can't wait to show you my new puppy and my doll collection! Papa bought me a doll at every city he visited when he was studying in America.'

The eight of us held a council, and carefully made our plans. We'd all dress in our school uniforms and gather in front of our school at eight. Wu Chun-mei's driver would meet us there and take us to her home. We felt very grown-up and conspiratorial.

I could hardly sleep the night before the party. On Tuesday morning, I put the silver dollar Aunt Baba had given me (for topping my class the previous term) in my pocket and walked to school with my book bag as quickly as possible. Wu Chun-mei's chauffeur was already there. We piled into Dr Wu's big American car, giggling all the way, and spent a wonderful morning playing with dolls, admiring Wu Chun-mei's puppy, eating watermelon seeds, skipping, and shooting basketballs into a hoop erected by Dr Wu in his garden.

I was watching Wu Chun-mei dribble the ball and admiring her shot sailing through the air into the net when her maid came out to summon us for lunch. It was twelve o'clock. I remembered with a sudden lurch who I was and where I was. For a few hours I had been a normal little girl attending a birthday party at her classmate's house. This was strictly prohibited and I had broken Niang's rules. If she found out, the consequences would be disastrous.

We walked towards the dining-room and everyone rushed off to the bathroom. I placed a restraining hand on Wu Chun-mei's arm and whispered, 'I have to go home for lunch. They're expecting me. I'll be right back.'

'Look what Mama has ordered the cook to make! You can't go now!' Wu Chun-mei said. Laid out on the dining-table were steaming baskets of meat-filled dumplings and bowls of noodles topped with barbecued pork and scallions. In the centre was an enormous birthday cake, colourfully decorated and piled high with whipped cream and eleven red candles.

'I really can't stay but I'll be back as soon as I can.'

'All right! What's your phone number?'

Without thinking, I replied, '79281. Don't look so disappointed. I'll be back before you cut your cake.'

'We'll wait for you!'

I ran home as fast as I could. The hall clock showed 12.09 as I dashed upstairs to use the bathroom. Normally, I would have arrived home at around 12.30. Wu Chun-mei's house was much closer than my school and I had overestimated the time. Never mind, better too early than too late. It just meant I'd have some time afterwards to buy her a birthday present with my silver dollar.

Bursting into my room in the highest spirits, I came face to face with Niang. She was standing by my desk in the bright sunshine, sleek and flawless in a brown dress covered with black spots. Her appearance reminded me of a leopard lying in wait.

My heart was pounding and blood was rushing into my temples and ears, beating over me in waves. A voice inside my head kept repeating, 'Be careful! Be careful!'

'Good afternoon, Niang!' I greeted her tremulously, fingering the silver coin in my pocket and wondering where to hide it. My tongue stuck to the roof of my mouth and I could hardly swallow.

'Why are you home so early?' she asked suspiciously.

'They let us out a little early,' I answered. She said nothing but continued to look at me unblinkingly, obviously expecting more of an explanation. 'From school, I mean,' I added stupidly, flipping the coin from one side to the other in my sweaty palm.

'What's that in your pocket?' she demanded, as if she could see through my uniform.

'Nothing!' I lied, squirming like a worm and wishing I could disappear.

'Come here!' she commanded. I approached her slowly, shaking like a leaf. She patted my body to search me, put her hand in my pocket and extracted the silver coin.

'Who gave you this?'

There was a prolonged silence. As I desperately searched for a plausible reply, all I heard was the buzz of a fly banging persistently against a window-pane.

'I am asking you a question!' she reminded me angrily. 'Where does this come from? I order you to answer me *now*!'

My brain was whirring but nothing came to mind. I looked dumbly at her cold, beautiful face. What could I tell her without implicating my aunt? I felt as trapped as the bluebottle whizzing around from pane to pane.

'Why are you home so early, you sneaky little liar? And where did you get this money?'

My silence was infuriating her. She took it as a personal insult, as if I was trying to provoke her. Her face suffused with rage, she slapped me. I felt dizzy and my ears hummed but I continued to stare at her in petrified silence.

'Until you give me a true explanation of what is going on,' she commanded, 'you will have nothing to eat or drink. I always knew no good would come of you!'

I opened my mouth. 'I . . . uh . . . I found the coin somewhere . . .' I lied vaguely, squirming around and hating myself. Inside, I was in complete turmoil with but one thought. I must not betray Aunt Baba.

'Did you steal something from the house and pawn it, you little thief?'

I was considering admitting to theft as a way out when we both noticed the new maid, Ah Sun, standing timidly at the door.

'Excuse me, Yen tai tai.' She cleared her throat nervously. 'There is a telephone call.' She nodded in my direction. 'For her.'

A new chasm had opened and I felt faint. I knew at once that Wu Chun-mei must have become tired of waiting for me to cut her cake. I kicked myself for carelessly giving out my telephone number.

Niang hurried down to answer the phone in the stairway landing. With a sickening feeling in the pit of my stomach, I heard her voice, now utterly transformed.

'My daughter is busy right now. This is her mother speaking. Who is calling please and can I give her a message?'

There was a short pause.

'Waiting for her to cut your birthday cake! How nice! Where is this celebration taking place?'

Another pause.

'But don't all of you have to be at school today? . . . Oh, I see! . . . A special holiday! . . . How splendid for you! . . . I'm afraid my daughter will not be returning to your party this afternoon. Don't wait any more!'

She came back and glared at me with scathing contempt. 'Not only are you a liar and a thief but you are manipulative as well. Nothing will ever come of you. The problem is that you have bad blood from your mother. You don't deserve to be housed and fed here. Girls like you should be sent away. You don't belong in this house!'

A shiver of ice ran through me. I felt my world crashing. 'You are to stay in your room without anything to eat until your father comes home,' she commanded.

Disgraced and miserable, I sat alone in my room looking down at Jackie restlessly pacing the garden. Time went by. I heard the sound of laughter and the clink of plates and cups drifting up from below. Afternoon tea was being served to Fourth Brother and Little Sister in their room, which we had nicknamed the antechamber. A while later, Fourth Brother appeared on his balcony carrying a plate of assorted goodies he no longer fancied. I watched him toss sausage rolls, chicken sandwiches and chestnut cake with nonchalance to a delighted Jackie, who jumped to catch the morsels between his powerful jaws. I drooled with hunger and longing as I imagined the delicacies sliding down my throat. Finally, I sat there with my eyes tightly shut, wishing with all my heart that when I opened them again, I would be Jackie and Jackie would be me.

Later, after Father returned home from work, he came into my room in a towering rage with the dog whip Hans (the dog-trainer) gave him last Christmas looped around his arm. When he questioned me I could not lie. He ordered me to lie face down on my bed and he whipped me. As I lay there trembling with pain and shame, I saw a rat scurrying across the floor, its eyes bright and alert and its long tail trailing behind. I almost screamed out in terror but bit my lip and remained silent throughout the punishment.

'Unfortunately,' Father announced, 'your aunt is a bad influence. She gives you money behind our backs and continues to spoil you. I'm afraid you two will have to be separated.'

I looked up at him in utter desolation. The fabric of my life was about to be torn apart. My heart felt heavy with the most excruciating pain. But he merely relooped the whip over his arm and walked out.

14. Class President
班 長

'WHAT happened to you yesterday?' Wu Chun-mei whispered as we took our seats in the classroom to begin our lessons. 'We waited and waited for you to cut the cake, only to find out from your mother that you weren't coming back . . .'

My face was still smarting from Niang's slaps. Was it my imagination or was my friend looking at me strangely? I couldn't help wondering if my face was bruised or swollen. Did she suspect something?

I opened my book and hid behind it as I muttered, 'Sorry. My mother wanted me to help around the house. You know how mothers are . . .'

I was searching desperately for a plausible excuse when Teacher Wong inadvertently came to my rescue.

'Yen Jun-ling (嚴君玲)! Wu Chun-mei! Stop talking at once and start paying attention!' she commanded in a loud voice. 'Now I want all of you to listen carefully. Tomorrow is a very special day because it is Election Day. Tomorrow is the day when you will cast your votes to choose your class president. Do you remember what your headmistress told you at general assembly two weeks ago? To refresh your memory, she has instructed me to read that part of her speech again.

'Being class president of your grade, the sixth grade, is a rare honour. To begin with, this year will be your final year at Sheng Xin Primary School. On graduation, most of you will go on to first grade at Aurora Middle School next door. Yours is the only class permitted to elect its president democratically: the same as in the United States of America. The head girls of all the lower forms are chosen by their form mistress. Only in your form, the sixth and highest form, do we allow a free election to be held. Instead of suggesting names to you, we grant you the right to nominate your own candidates. The winner will be president not only of your class, but the head girl of our entire school!

'The election will be held in our classroom during the first period tomorrow. I have brought some coloured balloons and large sheets of scrap-paper. During recess and for one hour after school today, you are permitted to stay in your classroom and blow up balloons or work on your campaign posters if you so desire. Let this be your first experience of "democracy in action".'

On hearing this, Wu Chun-mei and I looked at each other with dismay. When our headmistress first made the announcement two weeks earlier, my friend had immediately nominated me as a candidate and volunteered to be my campaign manager. However, her birthday had driven all else from our minds and we had forgotten all about it.

Unfortunately Chen Lei-lei, our chief rival, had not forgotten. Her father was a military general in the Nationalist army. She came to school every morning in a chauffeured black Cadillac complete with bullet-proof glass, escorted by an armed, white Russian bodyguard.

Between periods, Chen Lei-lei handed out chocolate bars, beef jerky, pencils and bookmarks to the whole class. I, of course, had nothing to give to anybody, not even to Wu Chun-mei.

During recess Teacher Wong wrote on the blackboard in big characters: TOMORROW IS FREE ELECTION DAY FOR CLASS PRESIDENT! COME AND CAST YOUR VOTES! We blew up balloons and hung them from window-ledges and overhead light fixtures. We wrote giant characters with brush and ink on huge posters – VICTORY! DEMOCRACY! FREE VOTE! – and stuck them to the walls. Our classroom looked colourful and festive. We were proud when we saw the lower-formers gawking enviously through the window.

When the bell rang at the end of our last class, Wu Chun-mei said, 'Yen Jun-ling! You'd better make a speech before everyone goes home. Teacher Wong said we could stay for one hour after school. Now is your chance!'

I was nervous but I knew I had to seize the opportunity. So I said okay. Wu Chun-mei climbed onto her chair and made an announcement. To our amazement, everyone stayed to listen, including Teacher Wong.

I tried to keep calm but my mouth felt dry and my heart was pounding as I changed places with Wu Chun-mei and stood on her chair.

'Fellow classmates!' I began. 'Wu Chun-mei has nominated me as a candidate for class president. She doesn't know this but I think *she* should be the candidate instead of me. Not only is she a natural leader and a superb linguist, she is also our school champion in shuttlecock, ping-pong and badminton. Compared to her, I am truly a nobody. My only attribute is that I have never been absent from school in the five years I've been coming here. The reason for this is because I love my school and prefer to be here than anywhere else in the world. If Wu Chun-mei is elected, I shall try to persuade her to donate some of her old books so that we can start a school library where we can go and read if we feel like it.'

There was applause and out of the corner of my eye, I saw Chen Lei-lei preparing to make her speech. I got down from my chair and whispered to Wu Chun-mei, 'I'm sorry but I have to go home now. I've already stayed longer than I should. My mother will be very angry if I'm late.'

'What's this about *me* being class president all of a sudden?' Wu Chun-mei asked.

'I meant every word I said. You deserve it more than anyone else.'

'We'll see about that! But do you really have to go? Can't you stay for another half hour?'

'I wish I could! You have no idea how much I would love to stay!' I had a sudden vision of Niang in her brown leopard's dress lying in wait for me in my room and felt breathless with terror. 'I am so sorry, I simply can't stay any longer.'

Something in my voice touched her. 'All right!' she said. But as I hurried out with my school-bag, she added, 'Don't worry! I'll win this thing for you! Afterwards, let's have a party in my house to celebrate. Mama says we still have a lot of cake left over from my birthday.'

I was so scared of being late, I ran all the way home. On entering the back door, I saw Ah Sun chopping vegetables in the kitchen. She stopped when she saw me and asked me to bring a thermos flask of hot water to my Aunt Baba.

'Is she home already?' I asked, delighted and surprised.

'Yes. She came back early. This water has just boiled and is piping hot. Wait here while I fill the flask and you can take it up to her for me.'

I crept upstairs with the thermos flask and my school-bag. Aunt Baba was sitting in an easy chair facing the garden and knitting. I put down everything quietly by the door, then tiptoed softly behind her and clapped my hands over her eyes. 'Boo!'

'Silly girl! I've been waiting for you. Ye Ye and I have just been talking about you. I came home so late last night we didn't have a proper talk. What did your father say to you yesterday after he whipped you?'

I looked at her lined, care-worn face; her kind eyes peering out from behind thick glasses; and her straight black hair combed back into a bun with white strands above her ears. Somehow, I found it difficult to tell her. Besides, I didn't really want to remember his words.

'Nothing! He didn't say much.' I busied myself pouring us each a cup of hot water.

'Close the door and come sit by me.'

'I have to do my homework.'

She smoothed my hair as I sat down at my writing table and set out my books. 'Tell me what your father said!'

'I just told you! He said nothing! Look! Leave me alone and let me do my arithmetic! Okay? I must study. It's very, very important.'

'Why are you getting angry?'

'I don't know! I want to forget about everything that goes on here. I love my school. There I have friends! There I have fun! We sit together and discuss books and things. My friends respect me. My teachers like me. They've nominated me for class president! Tomorrow is election day! Please don't ask any more questions!'

There was a knock on our door and Ye Ye entered. He regarded me with dismay as I lowered my head in shame at my outburst. I thought he would scold me but instead he turned to Aunt Baba. 'Let her study! She won't disappoint you. When you've reached my age, you know which children are weak and which are strong. Don't ask her too many questions. Don't criticise her or tear her down. I don't want her to grow up like Big Sister. She is going to be different!'

*

The next day started off with a bang. We couldn't wait to cast our votes! Although Teacher Wong had written the names of five nominated candidates on the blackboard, I knew my only true rival was Chen Lei-lei. The others were simply too disorganised.

Teacher Wong placed a large cardboard box on her desk. She passed out small sheets of paper on which we wrote the name of our chosen candidate. One by one, we walked up to insert our ballots in a slit in the middle of the box. After all the votes were cast, Teacher Wong shook the box and read out each name while we tallied the total in our notebooks. Chen Lei-lei, who had the best handwriting and topped the class in calligraphy, was ordered to write the number of votes against each candidate's name on the blackboard.

The results were close but in the end it was really Wu Chun-mei who won the election for me. Because of her athletic ability, she was very popular. Everyone wanted my friend on her team. By endorsing me instead of campaigning for herself, she was able to sway many who were undecided. Because she and I united and formed a team, we consolidated our votes and won.

All day we revelled in our success. Though I was a little fearful that Wu Chun-mei would again mention the party at her house after school, she said nothing more about it. I walked home as soon as school was let out.

It was a beautiful afternoon, sunny and cool. Avenue Joffre bristled with trams, cars, rickshaws and pedicabs. The jagged leaves on the giant sycamore trees lining the boulevard were turning russet and golden-brown in the autumn sunshine. I felt on top of the world as I bounced along the pavement, running and skipping now and then from sheer exuberance. What did it matter that I was a disgrace to my parents? How could anyone full of bad blood be elected class president? What was bad blood anyway? Niang predicted a hopeless future for me. Father said nothing would come of me. In spite of this, my classmates had chosen me as their chief representative. In her speech, Teacher Wong congratulated me on my triumph in our first election – democratically and honestly held – just as in America, the greatest country in the world. As she spoke, I thought, Though my parents tell me I'm worthless, I've proved them wrong! Of all the girls in my class, my classmates chose *me* to be their class president. I must forget about my home. In my other life – my real life – I'm not worthless. They respect me.

As soon as I entered my house by the back door, my happiness started to seep away. Cook and Ah Sun were in the kitchen cleaning a fish for dinner. They hardly looked up when I walked by. I greeted them with the news that I was now the newly elected president of my class. Their very posture reminded me that I was still in disgrace from the birthday-party fiasco two days before. Cook waved me on impatiently, obviously less than impressed by my victory. 'Can't you see we've work to do?' he asked brusquely.

I climbed the stairs and went into my room. When I closed the door and laid out my homework on my desk, the weight of the rest of the house seemed to slide off my heart. Shafts of sunlight flooded in from the large windows, exposing tiny particles of dust dancing in its wake. I took out my exercise book where today's votes were tallied, relishing once more the thrill of the contest and the triumph of my victory earlier that morning. Head girl of Sheng Xin! How sweet life was!

In a dreamy trance, I placed some water in the receptacle of my stone writing-tablet, grinding a stick of charcoal against its moistened flat surface to make fresh ink. I lubricated my brush and started on my calligraphy ...

There was a knock on the door and Ah Sun entered at once without waiting, looking flustered and fearful.

'A crowd of your little friends is downstairs in the living-room. They're asking for you,' she whispered.

Her words were like a thunderbolt out of a clear blue sky. I stared at her dumbfounded. 'Is my mother home?' I finally blurted out.

'I'm afraid she is. So is your father.'

'Tell my friends I'm not home. Please send them away!' I begged her desperately.

Ah Sun shook her head. 'I tried but they know you're here. Apparently they followed you home from school and saw you enter the door. They want to give you a surprise celebration party for winning the election for class president. Everyone has brought a gift. They mean well.'

'I know.' I felt panic-stricken but had no choice but to follow Ah Sun to the parlour. As I crept down the stairs, I could hear the giggles and screams of my classmates resounding through the entire house.

I bit my lower lip and forced myself to go in and greet my friends. They surrounded me, shouting 'Surprise! Congratulations! Victory!', singing and chanting slogans, drunk with euphoria and excitement. No one seemed to notice my tongue-tied silence. I shifted my eyes away from meeting anyone else's, afraid that my secret home-life was about to be exposed. Inside, I was quaking with terror, hoping against hope that Niang would leave us alone until I could politely ask my friends to leave.

Ah Sun reappeared and touched me on the arm. 'Your mother wishes to see you *now*!'

I fought against the panic surging within and forced a stiff smile onto my face. 'I wonder what *she* wants!' I said with a shrug, hating myself for the pretence. 'Excuse me for a moment.'

My mind was blank when I knocked on the door of the Holy of Holies. My parents sat side by side, in a little alcove overlooking the garden. I tried to close the door after me but Niang told me to leave it open. I stood in front of them with my head hanging and my eyes fixed on Niang's red silk slippers. I could hear, indeed we could all hear, the gleeful squeals of a dozen merry ten-year-old girls echoing through the entire house.

'Who are these little hooligans,' Niang began, her voice seething with anger, 'making such a racket in the living-room downstairs?'

'They're my friends from school.'

'Who invited them here?'

'No one.'

'What are they doing here?'

'They came to celebrate my winning the election for class president.'

'Is this party your idea?'

'No, Niang.' I shook my head in denial. 'They came of their own accord. I didn't know anything about it.'

'Come here!' she screamed. I approached her gingerly, trembling with terror. She slapped my face so hard I almost fell. 'Liar! You planned it, didn't you, to show off our house to your penniless classmates. How dare you!'

'No, I didn't.' Tears streaked down my cheeks and I found it hard to breathe.

'Your father works so hard to feed and clothe all of you. He comes home for a nap and there's not a moment of peace. What insolence to invite them into our living-room and make such a racket!'

'I never asked them here. They know I'm not allowed to go to their house after school so they decided to visit me instead.'

She slapped me with the back of her hand against my other cheek. 'Show-off! I'll teach you to be so sneaky!' she screamed loudly. 'Go downstairs this minute and tell your hooligan friends to get out! They are not welcome!'

As I hesitated and shuffled my feet, she hit my face yet again. 'Do you hear me?' she yelled at the top of her voice. 'I want them out of the house this minute! Are you deaf? Tell them to *gun dan* [get lost] and never come here again! Never! Never! Never!'

I clenched my fists and made my way slowly down the stairs. An eerie silence now permeated the house. My classmates must have heard Niang's every word through the open door of the Holy of Holies. My nose and eyes were drenched and I wiped them with the back of my sleeve. To my horror, I saw bright-red blood staining my hand and dress. Drops of blood trickled freely from my nose onto the floor. I realised Niang's blows must have caused a nosebleed and that my face was probably smeared with a mixture of blood, mucus and tears.

I re-entered the living-room and stood in front of my classmates unable to say a word. I felt naked and ghastly and vulnerable. None of them looked at me and I dared not look at them. At school, I had been so careful to pretend I came from a loving family. Now they knew the pathetic truth!

Unwanted and unloved by my own parents! How long did it take for a person to die of shame?

Finally, I choked out to the room at large, 'My father wishes to sleep. They want you to go home now. I am sorry.'

No one replied but, in the painful silence, Wu Chun-mei took out her handkerchief and handed it to me. I shrugged and tried to give her a smile of thanks but something in her eyes suddenly made it impossible for me to feign nonchalance. With tears strangling my voice, I told them, 'Thank you for coming. I'll never forget your loyalty.'

One by one they trooped out, leaving their gifts by my side. Wu Chun-mei lingered and was the last to go. As she filed past the stairway she shouted towards the Holy of Holies, 'This is unfair. You're cruel and barbaric! I'll tell my father!'

I gathered my presents and hesitated at the threshold of my parents' room, thinking about running away. Their door was wide open. Father ordered me to go in, close the door and unwrap my packages.

Out came a jumbled collection of comics, kung-fu novels, a chess set, a skipping-rope, packages of treats: salted plums, sweet ginger slices and dried watermelon seeds, and a sheet of calligraphy paper with the character VICTORY prominently stroked out with brush and ink.

'Throw the whole lot into the waste-paper basket!' Father commanded.

I hurried to comply.

'Why should your classmates give you gifts?' Niang asked suspiciously.

'It's because we won the election today. I'm now class president. We worked hard at it –'

Niang interrupted me in the middle of my explanation. 'Stop bragging!' she screamed. 'Who do you think you are? A princess of some sort that all your friends should come and pay you tribute? You are getting altogether too proud and conceited! No matter what you consider yourself to be, you are nothing without your father. Nothing! Nothing! Nothing!'

'You've breached our trust in you when you asked your friends to come here and insult us,' Father said in a quiet voice which made me grit my teeth in pain. 'Family ugliness should never be revealed in public. Since you're not happy here, you must go somewhere else.'

'But where can I go? Who will take me in?' I asked shakily.

'We're not sure,' Father replied cruelly.

Times were hard and on my way to school in the early mornings, I had seen infants wrapped in newspapers left to die in doorways. Beggar-children in rags routinely rummaged the garbage-cans searching for food. Some were reduced to eating the bark peeled off the sycamore trees lining the street on which we lived.

'What's going to happen to me? Will I be sold?' I knelt in front of them in a state of panic.

'You don't know how lucky you are to be fed and housed here in these uncertain times,' Father said. 'Apologise to your Niang.'

'I apologise, Niang.'

'It's your aunt who has taught you to lie and cheat. She feeds your arrogance by giving you money behind our backs,' Niang said. 'She is an evil influence. Before it's too late, you must move out of her room and not speak to her again. We'll find you an orphanage which'll take you in until you're old enough to find a job to support yourself. Your father has enough to worry about without the likes of you. You can go now.'

The thought of being separated from my aunt filled me with dread. Sombrely, I climbed the stairs and went back to the room I shared with her, perhaps for the last time.

After a sleepless night, I walked to school the next morning feeling apprehensive and ashamed. Along the way I kept asking myself, 'What'll my friends say this time? How will my voters look at me? Will I be the laughing stock of my class? Will everyone sneer and whisper about me during recess?'

I waited in the bathroom for a long time, reluctant to face my peers. When the bell rang, I was among the last to file into our classroom. Teacher Wong was already standing in front of the blackboard writing something with a piece of chalk. Immersed in my misery, I didn't pay any attention until Wu Chun-mei nudged me and pointed at our teacher's back. I looked and looked again. To my amazement, I saw my name (嚴君玲 Yen Jun-ling) written in big characters on the blackboard.

Teacher Wong turned towards me and smiled proudly. 'I want the class to welcome and salute Yen Jun-ling as your new class president. You have elected her of your own free will. From now on, she will be the one who will lead you in reciting Sun Yat-sen's last testament in front of our flag before lessons begin. When I am called away during class, she will take charge and you are to report to her!'

Everyone clapped and I glowed with happiness. The eyes of my supporters were shining with respect and admiration. I said to myself, How is it possible? Me, the same despised daughter publicly rejected by my parents yesterday is now being honoured by my teacher and classmates! Which is the true me? Though it's blatantly obvious that my father loathes me as much as my stepmother does, perhaps he'll change his mind one day if I bring him a few more honours. Besides, does he truly hate me or is he just going along with her because he loves her more than me and wants a peaceful life? After all, I *am* his real daughter.

All day, girls came up to offer their congratulations and pat me on my back. Nobody mentioned a word about being dismissed by my parents from my house. It was as if none of that ever happened. As I basked in their goodwill, yesterday's horrors started fading. By the time I walked home, I had put those dreadful memories behind and was light-heartedly skipping along the pavement from stone to stone.

I pushed open the back door and reality rushed back at once. Cook was plucking a freshly killed chicken in the kitchen. He glanced at me and called out ominously, 'Ah Sun, she's back from school!' Now why did he say that? I didn't wait to find out but my spirits sank and happiness evaporated as I climbed the stairs: past the Holy of Holies where the door was mercifully closed. Past the antechamber where my two half-siblings were having afternoon tea. (No tea for the likes of me, of course. Never tea for the likes of me!) Past my grandfather Ye Ye's room . . .

Ye Ye was standing at his door watching me with a sad expression on his face. He started to say something but Ah Sun was calling out in a loud voice, 'So you're back! Tell me what else belongs to you!'

She was in my room, kneeling on the floor and packing a suitcase.

'What are you doing?' I asked foolishly.

'What does it look like I'm doing? Your Niang ordered me to pack your clothes and move you out of your aunt's room. You are to sleep on the couch in your Ye Ye's room tonight. Tomorrow, your father and Niang are flying to Tianjin and you're to go with them.'

'To Tianjin tomorrow!' I exclaimed in dismay. 'And Aunt Baba, what about her? Is she coming too?'

'You must be dreaming! Your Niang says it's a bad thing you're always with her. She spoils you too much.'

'But I have homework to do!'

'Homework!' Ah Sun scoffed. 'What for when you're flying off in an aeroplane at noon!'

I ignored her and sat down at my desk, laid out my books and started my homework as if my life depended on it. As I tackled my maths and did my English translation, the gloom of tomorrow's departure seemed to lighten slightly. Ah Sun sneered at me, but I told her, 'This is what I want to do on my last afternoon in Shanghai.' She finished the packing and went away.

I sat forlornly at the edge of the landing on our floor, longing for my aunt to come home, desolate at the thought that I would never be able to go back to school or see any of my friends again. I pictured them waiting vainly for me to lead them in reciting Sun Yat-sen's last testament tomorrow morning; and I felt an overwhelming sense of despair.

For once, Aunt Baba was early. From the defeated way she walked up the stairs, I suspected she knew my fate. We entered our room and she closed the door. She peered over at my homework as she peeled off her coat.

'Autumn has come early this year and the weather turns chilly when the sun goes down,' she murmured, taking my cold hands and rubbing heat into them. 'Are you wearing enough clothes?' She looked for my sweater, fished it out of the packed suitcase and noticed a hole in the elbow. She found needle and thread and started her repair, her forehead creased in concentration.

She helped me put on my sweater. We sat side by side on her bed. She removed the key from the chain around her neck, opened her safe-deposit box and took out my stack of report cards. I knew that in her eyes, my grades had been conferred with an extraordinary value.

'Never mind!' she said consolingly. 'With such exceptional grades, you'll be able to become anybody you want! Let this be your secret weapon, your talisman, your magic charm which will bring you all the riches you can ever wish for. One day, the world will recognise your talent and we'll leave them and live together in our own home. Just the two of us.'

She didn't say how I should actually achieve this goal, seeing I was only ten years old and in the sixth grade and about to be banished to a Tianjin orphanage. I saw the mortified stoop of her shoulders and had no heart to challenge anything she was saying. I understood dimly the importance of both of us relishing the dream, though I could think of nothing but the heart-rending prospect of being sent away from her forever.

'Will you always be my aunt?'

'Of course!' She hugged me.

'Will you write to me every week?'

'Yes! And twice a week if you write to me too!'

'For always?'

'For as long as you're in Tianjin.' She hugged me again. 'And even after that, for as long as you'll remember me.'

'And then?'

'After that it's entirely up to you. I'll be here for you as long as I'm alive. Surely you know that? But you must never forget the dream. Try to do your best at all times. You have something precious and unique deep inside you which must not be wasted. I've always known that. You must prove them wrong! Promise?'

'Yes, I promise.'

15. Boarding-school in Tianjin
天津寄宿生

AT HONG-QIAO AIRPORT there were huge crowds milling around, pushing and shoving like a human tidal wave, fighting for tickets. To my amazement, fewer than ten passengers boarded our plane from Shanghai to Tianjin. I sat immediately behind Father and Niang next to an empty seat.

I didn't know it then, but the China I had always known was changing before my very eyes. My grandparents Ye Ye and Nai Nai were both born during the Qing Dynasty which ruled China for 267 years until Sun Yat-sen toppled it in 1911. Following Sun's revolution, local war-lords divided the country into fiefdoms and waged war with one another until the emergence of the Nationalist Party under Chiang Kai-shek. When Japan invaded in 1937, most of China was controlled by Chiang. However, the Communists under Mao Ze-dong were gaining momentum. Between 1937 and 1945, the Nationalists and Communists formed a united front to fight the Japanese. After Japan's surrender in 1945, the civil war resumed between Mao Ze-dong and Chiang Kai-shek for the control of China.

By September 1948, when Father and Niang took me north to Tianjin from Shanghai to separate me from my aunt, the Communists were already in control of Manchuria and were advancing rapidly southwards towards Beijing and Tianjin. Province after province was being lost to the victorious People's Liberation Army. Most people were fleeing in the opposite direction. Railroad stations, airports and dockyards were jammed with passengers wishing to escape to Taiwan and Hong Kong.

Being completely ignorant of the political situation, I merely thought it rather strange that the plane was so empty when the airport was so full. As soon as we took off, the airline hostess came around to hand out landing cards. 'Are you travelling alone?' she asked.

'No, I'm with my parents.'

'Good.' She smiled. 'Then they'll have to fill this out for you.'

Our aeroplane began to toss and roll. I felt sick to my stomach, closed my eyes and must have fallen asleep. When I awoke, Father was sitting by my side, gently shaking my shoulder. I sat bolt upright.

'Sorry, Father,' I began. 'Have we arrived?'

'Not yet.' He had three landing cards in his hand and a sheepish expression on his face. 'The stewardess asked me to fill out these cards. I'm afraid I've forgotten your Chinese name. Is it Jun-qing?'

A pang went through me. I meant so little to him, I was such a nobody that he didn't even remember my name! 'No, Father. That's Little Sister's name. Mine is Jun-ling.'

'Of course! Jun-ling!' He gave an embarrassed chuckle and quickly scribbled Jun-ling on the card. 'Now, give me your date of birth.'

'I'm afraid I don't know, Father.' It was true. In our family, the step-children's birthdays were unknown. We counted for so little that our birthdays were never remembered, let alone celebrated.

He scratched his head. 'Hmm . . . let's see now. How old are you?'

'I'm ten, Father.'

'Ten years old! How time flies!' He looked into space and was lost in reverie. After a while he continued, 'But we have to complete these landing cards! Tell you what. Why don't I give you my birthday? Would you like that?'

'Yes, please, Father!' How wonderful! To share the same birthday as my father! I was thrilled!

'Now you know what to say next time when someone asks you for your birthday.'

That's how November 30 became my birthday. The same day as my father's.

Niang's brother, Pierre Prosperi, met us at the airport. I had met him once before when he came to our home for dinner in Shanghai. I didn't know where I was or what time it was but dared not ask. The day seemed to be drawing to a close.

'Say good evening to your Uncle Pierre,' Niang instructed me. When I did, she exclaimed, 'Not in the Shanghai dialect! No one speaks that here.'

It was true. Everyone at the crowded airport was shouting to each other in Mandarin, the local dialect of Tianjin. Outside, it was already dark. I knew I was far from home, where Aunt Baba was probably having dinner with Ye Ye and my three brothers. Was she thinking of me too?

Father and Niang hurried me into a big, black motor car. Father sat in front talking business with Uncle Pierre and the chauffeur. Niang and I were alone in the back seat. I smelled her perfume and was dizzy with worry and nausea. I closed my eyes and pretended to be asleep because I was afraid. We drove for a long time. When we arrived, it was pitch black. The chauffeur got my suitcase out of the boot while Niang told me to stand with her in front of the massive gates of a large building. It looked vaguely familiar. Where had I seen it before?

The gates swung open as soon as Niang pressed the bell. Two tall foreign nuns in starched white habits were standing at the door. They shook Niang's hand and patted me on the head.

'We have been waiting for you,' they said.

'Bow to Mother Marie and Mother Natalie!' Niang instructed and I bowed obediently.

'Sorry we are so late!' Niang exclaimed as the chauffeur took my suitcase inside. 'Behave yourself and listen to the sisters!' Suddenly I realised she was speaking to me. More than that,

I was being dismissed. 'Mother Marie used to be my English teacher and Mother Natalie my French teacher when I studied here.' She turned to the sisters with a charming smile. 'I won't trouble you now but will telephone you at a more civilised hour tomorrow. Sleep well!'

She strode back towards the car, with the chauffeur trailing behind. He respectfully opened the car door for her, started the engine and pulled away. All this time, Father and Uncle Pierre had remained in the car, talking to each other in hushed, earnest voices. Neither of them bothered to look up or wave goodbye.

I watched the tail-lights of Father's car disappear and an awful loneliness sank in. They had tossed me aside like a piece of garbage.

The sisters spoke in English, which I barely understood. When I answered in Mandarin, they shook their heads. 'No! No! No Chinese! You must speak only English or French here! This is how you learn!'

They took me into a big room with rows and rows of beds, each with a curtain at its side. Only the three beds nearest to the door had their curtains drawn. Mother Natalie placed a finger against her lips for silence. She pointed to the bed next to the three occupied ones and closed the curtain softly. 'This is where you'll sleep, with the other three boarders here. We used to have so many and now there are only four, counting you. Tomorrow you'll meet them all. Come with me now and I'll show you the bathroom. It's late and you must be tired.'

'Where am I, Mother Natalie?' I asked. 'Am I in Tianjin?'

She stared at me in astonishment. 'Didn't your mother tell you? Yes! You're in Tianjin and she has enrolled you as a boarder at St Joseph's where she herself went to school. She telephoned us two days ago and told us you attended kindergarten here as a day girl when you were five years old. Don't you remember?'

I lay awake for a long time snuggled under the blankets, thinking. No wonder those iron gates looked familiar! So I'm back at St Joseph's. Well, at least I'm not in an orphanage. Things could be worse. Through a slit in my curtain I could see the shapes of the rows of empty beds in the semi-darkness. Bed after bed with no child sleeping. Each with its curtain primly pulled back, waiting and waiting. Every one bare and sorrowful. Just like me.

*

I must have dozed off because I woke to the murmur of voices. Sunlight poured through my curtain and I recalled with a start that I was in a strange place far from home. I crawled out of bed and nervously peered through my curtain.

A little girl my age was sitting on the bed next to mine talking to a grown-up woman. They smiled at me.

'Hello,' the girl said in English. 'Did you sleep well?'

'Yes!' I answered, adding hastily in Mandarin, 'My English is bad. In fact, I hardly speak any!'

She switched at once to Chinese and said, 'I am Nancy Chen. This is my mother. Mother Natalie says you flew in from Shanghai yesterday. Is that true?'

I nodded my head.

Nancy turned triumphantly to her mother. 'See, didn't I tell you?'

'I can hardly believe this,' Mrs Chen exclaimed. 'Aren't you afraid?'

'No,' I replied with a laugh. 'Afraid of what?'

'Didn't your parents tell you the Communists don't believe in God and hate foreigners? A Chinese student in a foreign convent school is seen by them as a member of the same religious order and will be persecuted along with the nuns if they win the war.'

I could only stare at her dumbly as she continued. 'What are your parents thinking of? Everyone is fleeing Tianjin for Shanghai or Hong Kong. And here you are coming from the opposite direction! Do your parents plan to move to Tianjin and live here from now on?'

'I don't think so. I heard Father say to my uncle in the car yesterday that they're flying back to Shanghai in four days.'

She looked at me, horror-stricken. 'And they are leaving you here by yourself? All alone in a foreign convent school? Don't they read the newspapers in Shanghai? Haven't they heard the Communists are winning the war? Soon PLA soldiers will be marching in from Manchuria. When they arrive they'll probably arrest us capitalists along with the foreign sisters and put everybody in prison. Thousands of refugees from up north are pouring into Tianjin every day to get away from them! It's almost impossible to get a plane or train ticket out of here! We've been waiting for two months!'

Suddenly I remembered the chaos at the airport yesterday and could only suck in my breath, sick with dismay.

Then she said, 'What have you done that your parents should wish to punish you like this!'

My new school seemed so different from my old school in Shanghai. To begin with, there were fewer than one hundred pupils in this enormous place meant for a thousand. We were divided into six classes, depending not on age but on our ability to speak English.

To my embarrassment, they placed me in the beginners' group. My classmates ranged from five to eight years old even though I was almost eleven. It was as if I'd never left kindergarten. Instead of algebra, I was doing additions and subtractions.

We were not supposed to converse in Chinese with each other at any time. So I said nothing at all unless the sisters addressed me by name. My classmates probably thought I was dumb because I was so much bigger but never raised my hand or volunteered to answer any questions.

In English conversation class one day, Mother Marie pointed to me to stand up and read aloud from *Grimm's Fairy-tales*. My mouth was dry and I knew my accent was terrible. Mother Marie mimicked my pronunciation and everyone snickered.

Finally she asked, 'How old are you?'

'Ten.'

'How do you feel about coming to school here?'

I looked around at my classmates, all of them smaller, younger, smarter and fluent in English.

'I feel old,' I told her.

'You mean like having one foot in the grave?'

All the girls chuckled. I looked up the word 'grave' with a fury of concentration in the English–Chinese half of my dictionary. Then I made a quick search for two other words in the Chinese–English section.

'Well, as I was saying, do you feel as if you have one foot in the grave?'

'Yes! And my other foot is on a piece of watermelon rind!'

There was loud laughter and a twinkle came into Mother Marie's eyes. 'So we have a comedian here! Tell me, what is your favourite book?'

I held up my dictionary. 'This book here! I can't live without it.'

Everyone laughed, including Mother Marie. 'And if you can have one wish granted, what would that be?'

'To receive a letter addressed to me. Just one letter. From anyone.'

Nancy Chen left Tianjin with her mother in the middle of November 1948. By then, the number of students had dwindled and we were all gathered into one single classroom, ranging in age from seven to eighteen. Every morning, fewer girls would show up than the day before. One by one they vanished, many without saying goodbye. By the middle of December, I was the only student left.

Three days before Christmas, Mother Marie gave me an assignment. I was to learn by heart a poem called 'A visit from St Nicholas'.

I didn't like the poem. It was too hard. I looked up all the long, complicated English words and translated them into Chinese, but the poem still didn't thrill me.

When I recited it, Mother Marie asked, 'Who wrote it?'

'Someone called Clement Clarke Moore.'

'Really! I wouldn't have guessed in a million years! Clement Clarke Moore is probably turning over in his grave! It sounds like nothing I've heard before. I thought you were repeating a Chinese poem!' I didn't feel so badly because she smiled while saying this and patted me on the head. Besides, we were all by ourselves in the classroom and there was no other student there to laugh at me.

Mother Marie was nice but she seemed at a loss as to how and what to teach me. In fact, all the sisters appeared somewhat bewildered and avoided looking at me directly whenever they happened to meet me in the corridors. They themselves darted around aimlessly all day in their black and white winter habits, silently clicking their rosaries. The atmosphere was eerie and strange. Our days were numbered and we were doomed. The Communists were coming! Everyone knew, but nobody talked about it.

Day after day, I would wander by myself from classroom to classroom because there was nowhere to go and no one to play with. I hated being by myself and missed my schoolmates terribly. All the rooms were empty. Rows and rows of desks and chairs and nobody anywhere. I would look at the white-washed walls hung with maps of China, Tianjin and France, stand in front of the blank blackboard filmed with chalk dust, stare at the crucifix above the door, sit at a desk scarred by thousands of cuts and pencil marks. The place had become a ghost town.

Once I wandered into the chapel after lunch and found it full of praying nuns. Apparently, this was where the sisters were spending most of their time. I knelt on a pew and looked at the majestic, high, vaulted ceiling. The statues of Jesus and the Virgin Mary radiated a special tranquillity as they peered out from the candle-smoke and incense-vapour floating upwards. I dared not breathe too hard, for fear it would all be blown away. Someone started playing the organ. The music enchanted me. For a few minutes I felt safe again, the way I used to on Saturday nights in Shanghai, when I'd snuggle deliciously in bed for hours and hours, knowing there was no need to get up early the next morning. Once more, I saw Ye Ye and Aunt Baba playing cards by my bedside. Everything was cosy, relaxed and comfortable. My aunt's hair was combed back smoothly into a bun which glistened under the lamplight. I heard again the rhythm of her voice intermingled with Ye Ye's laughter drifting across the room. What wonderful, soothing sounds! Then she tucked the blankets around me and lowered the mosquito net over my bed.

On Christmas Day, I ate dinner all by myself in the vast refectory. Sister Helene brought me an enormous plate of ham, beans and potatoes. Meanwhile, she was rushing in and out distractedly, bringing in one thing at a time: bread, water, butter, apple-sauce, salt, pepper. But she had neglected to give me a fork and I had nothing to eat with. One minute, she seemed glad I was still around for her to fuss over. The next minute she had forgotten all about me after saying she would bring me hot Christmas pudding for dessert.

I sat for ages pushing my food around on my plate. Outside I could hear the sound of a gramophone scratching out the sweet refrain of 'Silent Night' sung by an unknown soprano. I put my head against my folded arms on the refectory table and fell asleep.

Later that evening, I wrote a Christmas letter to Aunt Baba.

Dearest Aunt Baba,

I have been trying to think of what I should say to you because I don't want to worry you, but there is no other student in the school now except for me. I am the only one left. Just me and the sisters in this enormous place. Sometimes I can't help wondering

*what's going to happen when the Communists come.
Will they take me away with the sisters and put me in
prison too?*

*It is impossible to describe to you how I feel. I have
written to you so many, many times! And to Ye Ye and
Third Brother too. So far, there is no letter from
anyone.*

*Why don't you write? Why doesn't anyone send
me a letter?*

*I want you to drop me a line when you get this. I
can't imagine why you don't reply. You have no idea
what it's like. To be all alone here makes me very, very
sad. At night I lie awake for a long time and stare at
all the other empty beds in my dormitory, laid out
next to each other like little tombs.*

*I want you to send me your photograph so I can
place it by my bed. I would give everything in the
world to be with you and Ye Ye again back in
Shanghai.*

Don't forget me.

Day after dreary day went by. New Year came
and it was 1949. There was nobody to play with
and nothing to do. The sisters were far too
worried and preoccupied to fuss with me. Every
day was a free day. I spent a lot of time in the
library reading fairy-tales. Mother Marie had

given me a book for Christmas called *Paper Magic (Playing Solitary Games with Paper: Origami and Paper Cuts)*. Hour after hour, I learned how to fold and cut paper into aeroplanes, ships, flowers, monkeys and birds. I loved this book because my troubles seemed to vanish when I applied its magic.

I didn't dare ask Mother Marie too often whether I had any mail because the answer was always no. I didn't know then that Niang had instructed the nuns to stop all my incoming and outgoing mail and forward it all to her instead.

'Look, there is no point inquiring any more!' she told me one day. 'Believe me, if you get a letter, I'll shout it from the roof top and bring it to you at once! Even if you're asleep I'll wake you up!'

Then she looked embarrassed and gave me a piece of candy which she took from a small gold box in her pocket. 'This little snuff box is the only thing I have to remind me of my father,' she told me. 'He died in Nîmes three years ago. So you see, we all suffer in one way or another . . . Let us pray for each other.' In her voice I heard sadness and fear.

*

I was bouncing a ball against the wall in the school yard, sending it as high as I could and jumping up to catch it. I saw Mother Marie huffing and puffing towards me. She was waving her right arm and yelling, 'Adeline!* Adeline!'

Was it lunchtime already? I glanced at her as I bounced the ball hard, one last time. Back up it went! I tried to catch it as it came down but it landed on my head. It hurt a lot but I didn't want Mother Marie to notice so I acted as if it were nothing. What was she saying?

'Adeline! Your aunt is here to take you out of school! She is sailing to Hong Kong next week and wants to take you with her!'

My heart gave a giant lurch as her words sank in. For a dazzling moment, I knew with every fibre of my being that somehow, against all odds, Aunt Baba had come to my rescue! The whole of me was vibrating with joy and I ran as fast as I could towards the visitors' lounge, followed by Mother Marie.

I stopped abruptly at the threshold. In front of me was a small, mousy, foreign woman with dark

* The French nuns called me Adeline Yen instead of Yen Jun-ling at St Joseph's School.

brown hair, dressed in a Western suit. There was no one else.

'Adeline!' she smiled and greeted me in English. 'How big you've grown! Do you remember me? I am Aunt Reine Schilling, your Niang's older sister.'

I smiled back shyly, saying nothing. A black wave of disappointment swept over me.

'Come here! Don't be afraid! The last time we met you were still in kindergarten. It must have been six years ago when your Nai Nai was still alive. You were only four or five years old then. No wonder you don't remember!'

Something came over me. Great waves of anguish swelled up. I tried again and again to greet her, to be polite and say how grateful I was that she had come. Words choked me as I struggled, silently cursing my poor English. Then, to my great embarrassment, in front of Mother Marie and this stranger, I started to weep.

I hardly knew why I was crying. For the last few months, I had taken the blows as they came, with stoical fortitude. The pain of being torn from my aunt; the anxiety of seeing all my schoolmates disappear from St Joseph's; the perception of being abandoned and forgotten; the fear of being imprisoned by the Communists; the knowledge of my teachers' own terror and helplessness . . .

Of course, I had no words to describe any of this. Somehow, it was still desperately important to put up a front and keep up the pretence. Besides, Aunt Reine was stroking my hair and telling me not to cry. 'Hush now! Hush! Everything will be all right! It's a good thing your parents mentioned you were enrolled as a boarder at St Joseph's when they dined with us in September. Otherwise how would we have known? To think we might have left Tianjin without you! Now you can sail with us to Hong Kong next week. You can share a cabin with me and my daughter Claudine. She is nine. My husband Jean will share one with our son Victor who is ten. Your parents will be so pleased to see you. They fled to Hong Kong three months ago with Ye Ye and your younger brother and sister.'

For the first time since my arrival in Tianjin, the sisters allowed me to go out. We walked briskly towards Father's house on Shandong Road. Outside, it was bright, sunny and cold. The streets were deserted. There was very little traffic and few pedestrians. A truckload of soldiers in peaked caps and padded winter uniforms drove past us.

'People's Liberation Army!' Aunt Reine exclaimed. 'How young they are! None of these Communist soldiers look over twenty.'

I was shocked. 'Is Tianjin in Communist hands?' I asked in a whisper. 'Has Chiang Kai-shek lost the war?'

'Yes! With hardly a bullet being fired! Beijing is lost too. The Nationalists simply gave up and retreated south. Didn't the sisters tell you?'

'No, they never talk about the civil war. But all the girls are gone and I am the only pupil left. Thank you for rescuing me.'

'It's a good thing I suddenly thought of you. You see, we've been living in your father's house for the last few months and taking care of it for him. Since we're leaving, I tried to contact your Big Sister to keep an eye on the house. That's when I learned she and her husband have already escaped to Taiwan. Didn't your sister visit you to say goodbye before she left Tianjin?'

'I've seen no one since I came here last September. You are my first and only visitor.'

'Aren't you afraid? All by yourself like this?'

I heard the concern in her voice and was close to tears again. 'A little.'

She tried to reassure me. 'Everything will be fine from now on.'

'Where is Aunt Baba? Is she in Hong Kong too?'

'No, she chose to remain in Shanghai.'

'Does Niang know you're taking me with you to Hong Kong?'

'No, I haven't had a chance to write her.'

I was terrified and trembled with fear. 'May I please go to Shanghai instead of Hong Kong?' I begged.

'No, of course not! The Communists will probably be marching into Shanghai in a few months. Don't look so scared! You'll be safe in less than three weeks. After lunch, we'll come back in a rickshaw and get your belongings. What can be better than being with your parents and Ye Ye in their new home in Hong Kong?'

I dared not reply but thought, What can be worse? All the time I was quaking at the thought of what Niang would say when she saw me.

16. Hong Kong
香 港

WE THREE children were very excited when we walked up the gangway of the British flagship *China Star* and saw officers, crew and staff rushing around. A Chinese steward led the way and helped Uncle Jean and Aunt Reine with our luggage. Victor, Claudine and I lagged behind. The steward was tall and thin and towered over everyone. His head was completely bald and he walked with a pronounced limp.

As we followed them down a long, narrow corridor towards our cabins, all we could see was the steward's shiny scalp bobbing up and down under the dimly lit ceiling lights. Victor whispered to me, 'One thing about having no hair at all on your head, you always look neat!'

Though I was still feeling nervous and tongue-tied because it had only been three days since Aunt Reine took me out of St Joseph's, I laughed out loud. That was the effect Victor had on people. He and Claudine made me feel at ease as soon as I met them.

'Boys to the right and girls to the left,' Uncle Jean said. Our two cabins were directly opposite each other. Inside, everything was neat, bare and clean.

While Aunt Reine, Claudine and I were unpacking, there was a knock on the door. Victor stood there, grinning from ear to ear and wearing a bright-red and orange life-jacket.

'Why are you wearing that?' Claudine protested. 'Our ship hasn't even sailed yet!'

'In case the *China Star* starts going down. Then you'll really be sorry you're not wearing one yourself! Here! Let me show you something!' He parted the curtain and looked out of the round porthole. Our cabin was below deck. Outside we could see nothing but deep dark water. It did appear rather sinister and forbidding.

Claudine became alarmed. 'Mama, how often does a ship sink?' she asked.

Before Aunt Reine had time to reply, Victor quipped with a straight face, 'Only once!'

Aunt Reine and I could not help laughing in spite of ourselves. But then Victor did something my brothers would never have done. He took off his life-jacket, slipped it on his sister and showed her how to adjust the straps.

There were only two narrow twin beds in our cabin, each covered with a dark-blue bedspread tucked in tightly. At night, our steward brought in a tiny roll-out cot because there were three of us.

I assumed that the cot was for me. Though the mattress was thin and barely six inches from the floor, I didn't mind because it was a small price to pay for being rescued from the Communists. I was arranging the blankets and pillow when Aunt Reine put a restraining hand on my arm.

'Now, now! Remember what I told you on your first day with us. It's share and share alike in our family. Nobody is going to be treated differently. Come, let's draw lots to decide who will sleep on the floor.'

She tore a sheet of paper into three parts, wrote Bed 1, Bed 2 and Cot, then folded and placed them in a paper bag from which we made our picks, including Aunt Reine herself. Claudine picked first, came up with 'Cot' and slept there the entire time without protest.

That was how the Schilling family treated me during the time I spent with them. They made me feel like I was their third child. For the first time in my life, I did not automatically get the short end of the stick but was given an equal share, just like Victor's and Claudine's.

As we steamed southwards, the weather became noticeably warmer. The sea was calm and we three children spent much time playing hide-and-seek on the decks. Once Victor hid in a lifeboat for half an hour while we searched everywhere. Then he suddenly jumped out as we passed below him, scaring and delighting us at the same time.

'I am Sinbad the Sailor!' he cried. 'Don't you love the smell of the salty sea and the noise of the engines and everything about this ship?'

'What I love best is the library. Let's go there!' I told them.

The library was tucked away in a quiet, secluded corner next to a sun-drenched atrium. All the books were in English. Most of them were mysteries, romances and travel books. We browsed for a while until Victor found a stack of games. Claudine turned out to be a whiz at Monopoly. While we played, I could not help noticing how nice Victor was to his sister. Though he liked to tease her, he was gentle and protective at the same time.

For long stretches of time on that voyage, as we chased each other on deck, read books in the library, played games in the atrium or made paper-cuts from the book Mother Marie had given me, I actually felt I was part of the Schilling family and no longer the unwanted daughter who always came last.

At night, I would fantasise about being adopted by them, belonging to them and going off with them forever. How wonderful life would be if I did not have to face Niang ever again! Then I would remember my true status and my heart would be touched by ice.

It could be put off no longer. The dreaded day had arrived for me to come face to face with Niang. Our ship steamed into the dock at Hong Kong Harbour. We walked down the gangplank in search of a familiar face but no one was there to meet us.

Aunt Reine comforted me. 'It was so difficult to get our boat tickets and I couldn't be sure until the very last minute. By then it was too late to write to your parents. Two months ago I did send them a letter to say we were definitely coming to Hong Kong soon but didn't know the exact date. I'll go find a telephone to tell them we're here, and that you're with us, Adeline. They'll be so thrilled!'

Victor and Claudine groaned in unison, crushed at not being met. I breathed a sigh of relief but quickly pretended disappointment.

We hailed a taxi and squeezed in with all our luggage. Aunt Reine turned to me. 'I forgot today is Sunday. We're lucky because when I phoned your parents, I found everyone home! Including your father!'

I sat in the taxi in silent terror. The roads were clean and traffic was orderly. Our cab trailed a tall, double-decker red bus which stopped at a traffic-light.

Claudine wound down the car window. 'How hot and stuffy Hong Kong is!' she said. 'Look at the street signs, they're all bilingual with English on top and Chinese at the bottom but nothing in French.'

Victor answered in a superior tone. 'Of course there is nothing in French. Everything has to be in English because we are on British soil. Hong Kong has been a British colony for over one hundred years. It became British when China lost the Opium War. Look at the shop signs! They have English on them too!'

Having spent so much time together while sailing from Tianjin to Hong Kong, the three of us had become good friends. Victor addressed me: 'Let's continue our Monopoly game when we get to your parents' place. On board ship, I kept losing. Maybe my luck will change here. Will you show me how to make those paper-cuts and lend me that book Mother Marie gave you called *Paper Magic*? What a smashing book! You think your mother will let us have some big sheets of paper so we can make fleets of aeroplanes and platoons of soldiers? I'll paint designs on them in two different colours and we can play war-games with them. Won't that be fun?' I smiled and nodded. Victor didn't know that the make-believe Niang I talked about was very different from the real one we'd be facing.

All too quickly, our cab turned into a street marked Boundary Street and stopped opposite an imposing school building. Was I to be dropped off at another school so soon? A large sign above the gate read Maryknoll Convent School. No children were about and the gate was closed.

The cab driver asked me for his fare in Cantonese, expecting me to translate since I was the only one with a Chinese face. Aunt Reine answered in fluent Mandarin and paid him. Regarding her with new respect, he pointed to the freshly painted three-storey apartment building next to us and helped with our luggage. So they live opposite a girls' school, I thought. Is Little Sister enrolled there? How convenient for her!

Suddenly, Father, Niang, Fourth Brother, Little Sister and two maids were swarming around us. 'Hello! Hello! Hello! Hello! Welcome! Welcome!' Niang was embracing Aunt Reine and chattering away gaily in a mixture of French and English. 'We have been watching out for you from our balcony! Come in! Come in!' Her greeting appeared to include me though she neither made eye contact nor addressed me directly.

Father grinned from ear to ear and warmly shook Uncle Jean's hand. Fourth Brother hailed Victor and Little Sister was making conversation with Claudine. In the hubbub, they had forgotten me! I felt faint at my good fortune and lingered behind with the maids, helping them with the luggage.

I was the last to struggle up the stairs with my suitcase. Their flat was on the second floor. The front door was half open and I entered a hallway cum dining-room. Inside it was dim but I heard voices and laughter emanating from the living-room. I blinked to clear my vision and put my case down tentatively, pushing it closely against a wall to make it as unobtrusive as possible.

Someone coughed and I looked up, realising with a start that I was not alone. My eyes adjusted to the semi-darkness and there, standing quietly at one end of the oval dining-table against a small window, was my grandfather!

'Ye Ye!' I cried as my heart leapt with joy. I rushed across to stand by his side, knowing he had been waiting for me.

'Let me look at you,' he said, measuring my head against his chest. 'My, how you have grown! I do believe you're already almost as tall as your Aunt Baba. Tell me, did you top your class before you left Tianjin?'

I couldn't very well tell him about being the only student left in the entire school. Besides, I was a little shy because he sounded strange and familiar at the same time. There was something else indefinable about him which brought a lump to my throat. I looked down at my feet, unable to speak for a moment.

'Have you already forgotten how to talk in our Shanghai dialect?' he teased. 'Are you able to jabber away in French and English now? Take off your coat! Why are you wearing it when sweat is pouring down your face? I do believe you're still dressed for the bitter Tianjin weather! What is to become of you! Grown so big and still so little!'

His voice was full of love, bringing back memories long suppressed – of home and Shanghai and Aunt Baba. I took off my coat and sweater. Underneath I was still wearing the long-sleeved white blouse and dark-blue woollen skirt which were the winter uniform of St Joseph's and the only things that still fitted me. 'We'd better go in and join your parents now,' he said with a hint of reluctance, leading the way. 'Otherwise they'll be wondering where you are.'

Inside the living-room everyone was crowded around a glass coffee table. They made room to include us and gave Ye Ye the seat of honour while I squatted on the floor with the other children. Aunt Reine had a pair of scissors in her right hand. She took her coat and examined the buttons one by one. As we watched, spellbound, she selected a button, cut a knot and pulled a thread. Out emerged a sparkling diamond to glitter magnificently against the dark brown cloth of her winter jacket. Everyone gasped and Niang laughed out loud while clapping her hands like a child.

Aunt Reine repeated the process until there were eight precious stones glittering in front of us, dazzling us with their radiance and lustre.

'My entire diamond collection!' Niang exclaimed. 'How clever you are, Reine! Did anyone suspect?'

'There were a few hair-raising moments,' Aunt Reine replied with a smile. 'But let's not dwell on those in front of the children! Not only do you have your gems back, we also have rescued your daughter from Communist hands! This calls for a double celebration, *n'est-ce pas?*'

Though Aunt Reine was speaking of me, neither Niang nor Father looked in my direction. So far, they had not addressed me at all. Theirs was the gaze that glances but does not see.

'Champagne all around!' Father exclaimed, grinning from ear to ear. 'How can we ever thank you enough? May we invite you to the Peninsula Hotel for dinner tonight? They have recently employed a new chef who is excellent . . .'

During the ensuing commotion, Ye Ye signalled me to leave the room with him. 'When Aunt Reine phoned this morning and I heard of your unexpected arrival in Hong Kong,' he said, 'I ordered the maids to set up a cot in my room at once. While your Niang is in this euphoric mood, quickly unpack your bag and settle in before she changes her mind about your staying here. This flat is small and there is little room . . .'

'Thank you, Ye Ye.' I picked up my suitcase and followed him to his room. There was no need to say more. He did not elaborate and I asked no questions. We understood each other's predicament only too well. He strolled back to the living-room while I started to unpack. The new quality in his voice that hadn't been there before came back to me. What was it? The correct word dawned as I closed the lid of my empty suitcase. Of course! It was 'defeat'. Ye Ye had given up.

The Schilling family stayed at a small hotel nearby. Next morning, they walked over for breakfast at nine o'clock. Father had already left for the office and Fourth Brother and Little Sister were at school. Niang made plans to take her sister's family shopping and sightseeing. She invited Ye Ye to accompany them.

'No thank you,' Ye Ye declined politely. 'I am feeling a little tired today. My neck bothers me.'

'Adeline, you can make yourself useful for once and massage Ye Ye's neck for him,' Niang ordered, looking directly at me for the first time.

I was overjoyed! Not only had Niang finally acknowledged me, she had even given me a task to perform! Perhaps she had forgiven me? 'Yes, Niang,' I answered promptly.

Victor groaned. 'Does that mean Adeline won't be coming with us? *Quel dommage*! Before I go, Adeline, how about folding a few more paper aeroplanes with me? There is still time.'

After their departure, Ye Ye and I settled comfortably in the airy and bright living-room.

'Read me the newspapers,' Ye Ye said. 'The newsprint here in Hong Kong is definitely smaller. I can hardly read the papers even with glasses. My doctor says it's due to my diabetes. Lately, I'm also having trouble hearing. My lower back aches as much as my neck. The worst thing about growing old is that the gadgets of my body are failing one by one.'

I started to read but all the news was depressing.

'It is estimated that the loss incurred at the Battle of Huai Hai has cost the Nationalists over half a million troops. Chiang Kai-shek has definitely resigned as president of China. Vice-president Li Tsung-jen takes office and is trying to negotiate peace with the Communists. People's Liberation Army soldiers are marching towards Nanking and Shanghai and are preparing to cross the Yantze River en masse. Mobs intending to flee Shanghai for Hong Kong and Taiwan congregate and riot for tickets at shipping offices. One US dollar is now worth 9.5 million Chinese yuans.' I stopped often because many Chinese words were unfamiliar.

'You are forgetting your Chinese!' Ye Ye admonished. 'Go get the dictionary on the table by my bed. Look up those new words I just taught you and copy them into your notebook.'

My mind was full of gloomy thoughts and I suddenly burst out, 'I'm sick and tired of blindly copying Chinese characters over and over into my notebook like a robot! I hate studying Chinese!

It's a waste of time. Besides, your dictionary is not a real dictionary. It's only a Chinese–Chinese dictionary, not a Chinese–English dictionary. I only want to learn English, not Chinese.'

'How can you say that?' Ye Ye exclaimed.

The hurt on his face made me cringe but I was unable to stop. 'My teacher Mother Marie says the only way to succeed in the second half of the twentieth century is to be fluent in English.'

'Hand me a piece of paper, get me a pen and come over here,' Ye Ye said softly. 'Let me show you something. Though you have a fine mind and a subtle intellect, the sentiments you express not only expose your ignorance, they also wound my heart. You forget that I know you only too well. Not only what you look like outside, but also how you are made inside. How can you say you hate the study of Chinese when you are Chinese yourself? Go look in the mirror if you have any doubts!

'You may be right in believing that if you study hard, one day you might become fluent in English. But you will still look Chinese and when people meet you, they'll see a Chinese girl no matter how well you speak English. You'll always be expected to know Chinese and if you don't, I'm afraid they will not respect you as much.

'Besides, China is a huge country with a vast population and an ancient culture. Though life has to be lived forward, it can only be understood backward. Reading Chinese history will enlighten you in ways no English writing can.

'I predict that in a hundred years from now, the world's many languages will be distilled down to three: Chinese, English and Spanish. Chinese will never disappear because China's population has a unified written language.

'Above all, there is the wisdom and magic of our language itself. When you read a Chinese book, try to look at the characters and think about them. I have met many who appear to know a good many Chinese words, but never actually grasp the true meaning of any of them.

'Let me give you the example of just one character 貝 (bei) to illustrate my point.

'In ancient times, cowrie shells were used as units of money and were exchanged for goods and services. In time, a hole was drilled in these shells and a row of shells was held together by a string. A string of shells was called 貝 (bei). Look at the character 貝 (bei) carefully. Does it not resemble a row of shells held together by a piece of string knotted at the end?

'I agree that Chinese words are more difficult to learn than English. We do not have an alphabet and there is no correlation at all between our written and spoken language. In fact, I once met a Frenchman who could not speak a word of Chinese but wrote and read Chinese so well he worked as a translator of Chinese law at the French consulate in Shanghai. Chinese is a pictorial language, not a phonetic one. Our words come from images. The meaning of many characters is subtle and profound. Other words are poetic and even philosophical.

'To go back to 貝 (bei). Because the word evolved from something that was "valuable" in ancient times, modern Chinese words containing the component 貝 (bei) are associated with finance or commerce in some way. Take the word 買; it means "to buy". 賣 means "to sell". Place the two words side by side 買賣 (buy-sell) and the term means business. Now, what is the essence of business if not buy-sell? Regardless of what commodity you are trading, if you wish to be successful in business, you hope to buy low and sell high. Otherwise you are in big trouble. This is universally true regardless of what business you're in.

'Look at 買 賣 again. What is the only difference between the two characters? Compared to 買 (buy), the word 賣 (sell) has the symbol 土 on top. What is 土? The word 土 means earth or land. If the essence of business is buy-sell, then its most important ingredient is 土 (earth or land). Should you go into business one day, keep this in mind. Everything else can be made better or cheaper or faster, but not land. It is the only commodity that can never be duplicated or replaced.

'Now look at two other words which also contain 貝 (bei). They appear very similar. At first glance, if you are careless, you might even mistake them for each other: 貧 (pin) and 貪 (tan). But you have to be very, very careful. Don't ever mix them up just because they resemble each other. 貧 (pin) means poverty. 貪 (tan) means greed. Remember how much the two words look alike. Yes, greed and poverty are intimately linked in mysterious ways indeed. All covet, all lose.

'You have the newspaper in front of you. Pick another word, for instance 意 (yi). Look at it. The top part 音 (yin) is "sound". The bottom part 心 (xin) is "heart". Does 心 not look like a jumping heart? Put 音 (yin) on top of 心 (xin) and you have 意 (yi) which means "sound from your heart". The new word 意 (yi) is the symbol for "intention" or "meaning". What is "intention" but a "sound from your heart"?

'How about a new word, a difficult word 繭 (jian). On top is the symbol for grass or straw or vegetable matter 艹. Below is a little house with a partition in the middle 巾. On the left of the wall is 幺, a symbol for small. On the right is 虫 (chong), a sign for worm. So here we have a little house made of vegetable matter with a little worm in it. What is the word? 繭 Cocoon! Look at it again. Now close your eyes! Do you see the little straw hut with a small worm inside?

'Then you can have two or more words which, combined together, are transformed into something wonderful and illuminating. For instance, 危 (wei) means danger. 機 (ji) means opportunity. Add them together and you have a "crisis" 危機. Break them apart and keep in mind: whenever you are in a crisis, you are in the midst of danger as well as opportunity. Now, do you still think the study of Chinese is boring?'

For a whole week, Niang went out with the Schillings. She always invited Ye Ye but never included me. Everyone knew she didn't really want Ye Ye to accompany them and only asked him out of politeness. He invariably thanked her and said he preferred to rest at home.

Did I mind being left behind with my grandfather? Of course not! As soon as Niang left, it was as if a heavy weight was lifted off my shoulders. Aside from Ye Ye, me and the maids, even the flat itself seemed to breathe a sigh of deliverance. At once, the whole place became brighter, cosier and friendlier. To the two of us sitting side by side playing Chinese chess or reading the newspaper, the house would gradually transform itself into a happier and more intimate place.

A week went by and it was Sunday again. The sun was shining, everyone was home and excitement was in the air. At breakfast, Niang announced, 'Today, we'll all go for a long scenic drive and visit the elegant Repulse Bay hotel on the far side of Hong Kong island. I've made lunch reservations at the hotel's dining-room where the view is breathtaking and the food delicious. Our car will travel from Kowloon to Hong Kong across the harbour by ferry. After lunch, we'll go for a swim at the beach, rent a tent and have an afternoon picnic. Won't that be fun?'

She made it sound so enticing that for once, even Ye Ye agreed to go.

I wondered if I was going to be included in this special outing. Niang had not said I couldn't go. Nor had she said I could.

One by one, they piled into Father's large Studebaker while the maids stocked the car boot with picnic hampers, lotion, blankets and towels. Father, Ye Ye and Uncle Jean sat in front. Niang, Aunt Reine, Claudine, Fourth Brother and Little Sister were in the back. Victor and I stood hesitantly next to each other. The car sagged under the weight of its many passengers.

'Come on, Victor,' Niang cried out gaily in French. 'Room for just one more, I think. We can all squeeze in just a little tighter.'

Victor was half in and half out of the car. He turned around and saw me watching him from the kerb. 'It's not fair, Maman. What about Adeline?' he asked Aunt Reine in French. 'Since Ye Ye is coming with us, she'll be home by herself. Why don't we take her along?'

Not understanding French and impatient to depart, Father asked Victor in English, 'What is it, Victor, do you want to use the bathroom before we start?'

Victor shook his head, 'No, Uncle Joseph,' he began in English but Niang interrupted him in French. 'There is not enough room. You can see how crowded we all are.'

'Then what about yesterday and the day before and the day before that?' Victor persisted.

'Stop dawdling and get in the car!' Aunt Reine commanded. 'Everyone is ready to go and you are delaying everything.'

'It's so unfair,' Victor continued. 'Why doesn't she get to go anywhere with us?'

'That's just the way it is!' Niang exclaimed sharply. 'You either get in now and come with us, or you can stay home with her. Suit yourself!'

'In that case,' Victor replied gallantly, 'I think I'll stay and keep Adeline company.'

He climbed out to stand by my side. Together, we watched the car drive off. I was overwhelmed by his chivalry but could find no words sufficient to express my gratitude. After a painful pause, I ran upstairs, dug out my book *Paper Magic*, gave it to him and said, 'This is for you.'

He took the book gingerly, too stunned to say a word, unable to believe his good luck.

17. Boarding-school in Hong Kong
香 港 寄 宿 生

I KNEW the Schillings were leaving Hong Kong for Geneva on Thursday morning, so I got up early and hovered around the front door, hoping Father would take me along when he left to drive them to the pier. But he was in a rush and I was too shy to say anything. The result was I never got to say goodbye.

Two days later, an hour after lunch on Saturday afternoon, the maid Ah Gum knocked on our door. I opened it softly and placed my finger against my lips because Ye Ye was taking his afternoon nap. She whispered that Niang wanted me to pack my bag immediately because I was being taken away.

Father was at the office and Little Sister was attending a birthday party. Niang, Fourth Brother and I climbed into the back seat of Father's Studebaker. I didn't know where they were taking me and dared not ask. In the car, Fourth Brother deliberately snubbed me. He was playing with Niang's diamond ring, twisting it round and round her finger. I envied his privilege and freedom as he nonchalantly positioned her finger this way and that, trying to catch the sun's rays. She looked on indulgently while I sat primly in my corner, with my back straight and my skirt pulled down, hoping to be unnoticed. I knew Fourth Brother was angry at me because of what had happened earlier.

Ye Ye had a habit of going into the living-room at eight o'clock every morning to read the newspapers before breakfast. His sight was failing and he liked the bright sunlight at that hour. To my surprise, I caught a glimpse of Fourth Brother lurking furtively in the hallway. I thought, It's Saturday and there's no school. Besides, Fourth Brother hates to get up early. What *is* he up to?

Now Ye Ye was shuffling slowly from the hall towards the half-open door of the living-room. I happened to look up and suddenly spotted a pile of thick encyclopedias propped precariously on the door's upper ledge: lying in wait, like their perpetrator Fourth Brother, to fall on Ye Ye's shaven head.

I was seized by a sudden rage. It was a sizzling hot day but I felt a chill within. In a flash, I lurched forward, overtook Ye Ye and pushed the door open violently. Three heavy volumes crashed to the floor, narrowly missing our heads and landing with a loud bang!

'Mind your own business!' His plans thwarted and beside himself with fury, Fourth Brother was screaming at me at the top of his lungs, '*Gun dan*! 滚蛋 [Get lost! Drop dead!].'

'How mean you are!' a voice declared. We both turned to see the tiny figure of Little Sister, arms akimbo, glaring at Fourth Brother from the doorway of her room.

Before either of us could react, Father rushed out in his bath-robe. Grasping the situation at once, he hesitated briefly. I saw his face, half turned towards Fourth Brother and half turned to return to his room. 'Pick up the books!' he commanded finally in a stern voice. 'Such a racket! Don't you know your mother is still sleeping?

Keep your voices down when you play! That goes for all three of you!'

And that was all.

Afterwards, Ye Ye and I sat by ourselves on the long couch not saying a word. I looked at my grandfather, defeated and resigned with a blanket around his drooping shoulders in the blistering heat, his face contorted with sadness and anguish. A tired old man with no one to turn to, imprisoned by his love for his only son, my father.

I closed my eyes and made him a promise. I didn't dare say it out loud but I wished very hard over and over, 'It's bound to get better. One day things will be different. Life won't go on like this forever. I don't know when, how or what but I'll come back and rescue you from this. I promise!'

In the car, Fourth Brother demanded to have afternoon tea at the posh Peninsula Hotel. We stopped there though I felt sick to my stomach, besieged with unknown fears but too afraid to utter a single word. As we approached the grand entrance, I spied a little girl standing forlornly beside a man kneeling on the ground with his head bowed. Both were in rags. On the pavement was a sheet of paper describing their miseries and a plea for help. The child had a large placard hanging around her neck on which was written, 'My name is Feng San-San. I am for sale'.

In the cool, luxurious lounge on the ground floor of the hotel, there was a long line of Chinese customers waiting to be seated for afternoon tea. The head waiter was writing down their names in a large leather-bound appointment book.

Fourth Brother had run ahead and was in the process of giving his name. As I approached with Niang, I heard the head waiter repeating in Chinese, 'Last name is Yen. Party of three? Looks like half an hour's wait, I'm afraid.'

Meanwhile, Niang was impatiently checking the time on her gold Rolex watch. Haughtily, she demanded in English to be seated immediately. 'My name is Prosperi,' she proclaimed in her best European accent. 'We are in a great hurry!'

With one sweeping glance, the head waiter took in Niang's French designer suit, alligator handbag, matching shoes and seven-carat diamond ring. 'Of course, madam,' he said, without any change of expression, while leading us past the long queue to sit at a table by the window. After all, Hong Kong was a British Colony. White people took precedence over the native population and went automatically to the head of every line, wherever that might be.

After tea, we crossed the harbour by ferry and drove past an impressive building, Governor's House, which was surrounded by lush green lawns and guarded by tall, English soldiers. Our car stopped at a large school building perched halfway up a slope. A sign outside said Sacred Heart School and Orphanage.

Two foreign nuns in white habits greeted us. Niang and Fourth Brother followed them into a conference room while I was left outside in the hall. Nobody was around and there was nothing to read except the school brochure lying on the table. Surely they couldn't fault me for perusing that!

I found out there were 1200 students enrolled at Sacred Heart, of whom sixty-five were boarders. The rest were day-girls. More ominously, Sacred Heart also had an orphanage for unwanted daughters abandoned by their parents. I felt my heart pounding as I pondered my fate.

I told myself: the danger is very real. Niang loathes me. As for Father, he doesn't really care. He hardly knows I exist, remembering neither my name nor my date of birth. To him I don't matter.

Finally, after one and a half hours, they emerged together. To my astonishment, Niang actually introduced me with a smile to Mother Mary and Mother Louisa. I thought: is this part of her trick to abandon me in the orphanage where I would cost her nothing? I had better concentrate on what she's saying. Good heavens! She is congratulating me on my good luck because the sisters are making an exception. I am being admitted as a boarder even though it's the middle of the school year! Did she say *boarder*? My heart is singing and I can hardly believe my good luck. There *is* a God after all!

18. Miserable Sunday
討 厭 的 星 期 天

Two years later. Summer, 1951

DURING mass at the cathedral I kept thinking, It's Sunday again and I feel so blue. There's no doubt about it. Sunday is my least favourite day of the week. Just thinking about it makes me cringe! Thank goodness it's the last Sunday of the summer term.

After mass we dashed into the refectory for breakfast. As usual, Mother Mary wheeled in a huge vat of steaming boiled eggs on a cart. These eggs were precious because you couldn't just order them from the sisters, no matter how rich your father was. Someone from home had to care enough about you to take the trouble to bring fresh eggs to you personally, carefully wrapped and padded in newspapers, during visiting hours on Sundays. In addition, you had to paint your school-number in indelible ink on the shell and retrieve your egg when Mother Mary called your number during breakfast. Then you walked back to your seat with your egg perched proudly in your egg cup, showing the whole world that you were cherished and beloved.

Since no one had ever come to visit me (let alone brought me an egg), it was humiliating to sit there morning after morning looking on, knowing my number would never come up. During these sessions, I usually pretended to be deaf and preoccupied.

Suddenly, my friend Rachel shoved my elbow. 'Do you hear what I hear, Adeline? Mother just called your number! 37!'

'Impossible!' But sure enough, I heard Mother Mary plainly this time. 'Number 37!'

I rose with amazed delight. The whole refectory was now silent. All eyes were watching me. Nobody believed my number had been called. Nor did I!

I returned with my prize settled in its very own cup. First time in two years! Finally an egg after 730 eggless mornings! Carefully, I examined its surface. The number 37 was plainly visible, painted in black ink on the smooth, brownish shell. I thought, Who is it from? Do I have a secret admirer? Dare I eat it? Is it really mine to be consumed at will?

I imagined tapping my egg with the back of my spoon, cracking its top, delicately peeling off the broken bits of shell and digging into its white membranous surface. Oh, what bliss to taste that wonderful rich yolk on my tongue and let it slide deliciously down my throat! So very, very tempting! I longed for it. Yet I knew very well it was not mine. It was a mistake. Perhaps a trick or a cruel practical joke. What if the rightful owner came up while I was in the middle of enjoying my egg and claimed it? What should I do then? Once I broke the shell, there was no going back.

I steeled myself and got up from the table. Mother Mary had just handed out the last egg and was about to leave with her empty vat. I approached her hesitantly, feeling confused and defensive, and handed back the egg.

'Mother Mary! This is not mine.'

Impatiently, she dropped the vat and scrutinised my egg with a sigh. 'It says 37. What is your number? Are you Number 37?'

'Yes, Mother!'

'Then the egg is yours.'

'No, it can't be!'

'Why not? Why can't it be?'

Everyone had stopped eating and was listening intently. There was not a sound. This is terrible! I thought. I'm drawing attention to myself and broadcasting my state of perpetual egglessness. What can I say that's logical and convincing and still preserve a bit of dignity?

'My parents know I *hate* boiled eggs. That's why they never bring me any,' I blurted out, my face burning with shame at the lie. 'So there is no possibility this egg can be mine!'

Behind me, I heard someone (probably Monica) snickering and saying in a loud stage-whisper, 'I suppose she hates chocolates and mangoes too. That's why no one ever comes on Sundays to bring her any goodies at all.'

Sixteen-year-old Monica Lim was three years older than I and the daughter of one of the richest tycoons in Hong Kong. She was tall, pretty and well groomed. Her nickname was 'Brains' because she routinely topped her class. Rumours were she'd be head girl next year.

Every Sunday, Monica dressed in the latest European fashion to greet her mother, who reputedly was not her illustrious father's real wife but merely a concubine and a former bar-girl. During visiting hours on Sundays, the only day we boarders were allowed to dress in street clothes, Monica and her mother looked like models as they strutted around the school yard in fashionable costumes, embellished with padded bras, silk stockings, tailored qipaos and imported high-heeled shoes. Besides eggs, her mother brought Monica soda crackers, Maltesers, Cadbury chocolate bars, beef jerky, seasonal fresh fruits and Dairy Farm ice-cream. On her birthday, Monica traditionally got a giant cream cake covered with luscious strawberries which she shared only with certain hand-picked, chosen 'friends'. Because of her father's fabulous wealth, she was much pampered by the nuns and received many special privileges.

For a long time, Monica had ignored me. She was one of the elite group of beautiful 'big girls' whom we plain 'little ones' were supposed to admire and worship from afar. Then we both got picked to write for the school magazine. In three successive issues, my essays were selected over hers by Mother Agnes, our editor. At the end of my first year at Sacred Heart, I skipped a grade and the girls started calling me 'scholar'. They began comparing my writing to Monica's. One day, I accidentally bumped into her in the library and she said resentfully, 'Instead of trying to memorise every book in here, you'd be more popular if you got yourself some pretty dresses instead.'

I felt my face go hot because I knew I looked terrible. Having no money and not knowing where to buy a bra I tried to hide my budding breasts by wearing two sets of shrunken underwear to flatten my chest. Besides my uniforms, I possessed only one old-fashioned plain brown Sunday dress which was too small, too short and too tight. I always wore tennis shoes because those were the only shoes available for sale in the school gym and Mother Mary had permission to charge them to Father's account at her discretion. As for my hair, well, I knew I'd better not even think about it! So I swallowed my anger and walked away. In spite of Monica's unkind remark, the girls ignored her and nobody else made fun of me.

Towards the end of breakfast, Mother Mary announced that because it was the last Sunday before the beginning of summer holidays, visiting hours were being extended from two to three hours. Everyone cheered, but I felt jittery. When I'm nervous I always have to go to the bathroom. It was crowded with everyone preparing to meet their parents. They were preening themselves in front of the mirror and arranging their hair. Not yet! Better wait another half hour. I sauntered into the library and picked out a few books. What a beautiful room! Away from all the noise, giggles and excitement. My haven. My sanctuary. The place where I belonged! My real world!

But even here, I didn't feel entirely safe on Sunday mornings. It was okay for a temporary respite, but girls sometimes brought their parents in for a tour of the premises. When they saw me they felt obliged to make polite conversation, though I'd much rather they ignored me and treated me as part of the furniture. Sure enough, my classmate Irene Tan walked in with her mother.

'This is our library, Mother. Oh hello, Adeline. Let me introduce you to my mother! This is Adeline Yen, top student of our class. She skipped two grades and will be going into Form 5 after the holidays, at 13!'

'Studying so hard even on a Sunday!' Mrs Tan exclaimed, turning to her daughter. 'Now, why can't *you* be like that?'

I felt like a freak and looked enviously at Irene's elegant new sandals and matching dress. 'No! No! I'm not studying. This is purely for pleasure and recreation.'

Mrs Tan came over and glanced at my book. 'What are you reading? *King Lear*! My! My! You say *this* is for pleasure?'

I hung my head and saw my worn tennis shoes with the hole at the side and wrinkled stockings with the elastic washed away, knowing I must appear very odd indeed in my old-fashioned, tight, shabby brown dress next to Irene's stylish elegance. Hanging about in the library and reading *King Lear* from choice simply rounded out the whole dismal picture. A special sort of idiot savant found in Hong Kong Catholic convent schools. I was wishing fervently I could disappear when I heard Irene say,

'Last Friday we were reading *King Lear* out loud in class and Adeline suddenly burst out crying.'

I felt an intense heat spreading upwards from my neck. What she reported was true but I had no words to explain it away. The poetry and pathos of *Lear* had moved me so profoundly I simply couldn't control myself. So much of his plight seemed to mirror that of my grandfather's at home. Contrary to all logic, I had the uncanny sensation that Shakespeare had actually had my Ye Ye in mind when he wrote his immortal play four hundred years earlier.

When Lear knelt in front of his evil daughter Regan to plead for his food and lodging I saw my Ye Ye dropping to his knees to say the same terrible words to my stepmother,

> *Dear daughter, I confess that I am old*
> *Age is unnecessary: on my knees I beg*
> *That you'll vouchsafe me raiment, bed and food . . .*

However, Mrs Tan was looking at me with an odd expression on her face: halfway between pity and curiosity. It made me acutely uncomfortable. All I wanted was to make a quick getaway.

I glanced at the clock and feigned surprise. 'Oh! Excuse me! Is it 10.15 already? I'd better go get ready. Otherwise I'll be late!'

I strode out purposefully with an armful of books though I didn't know where to head for, hating myself for my pretence. Why couldn't I tell Mrs Tan candidly, 'I hide out and read in the library because my parents never come to visit me. And I don't like everyone to notice I'm the only one always left out. It's easier to make myself invisible. I wish I had someone like you. Irene is very lucky.'

Tentatively I circled the bathroom. In American magazines, they described it as 'casing the joint'. Thank goodness it was now deserted. Furtively, I walked away at first, then retraced my steps and quickly slipped into the last, most unobtrusive lavatory cubicle. I locked the door and carefully placed my stack of books on a ledge by the window, so that nobody would see them should anyone peek under the gap beneath the door. I ensconced myself on the toilet seat with a sigh of relief. It was smelly and damp but I felt safe. No one could get at me. Privacy at last! No prying eyes, spiteful remarks, pitying glances. I was alone with my beloved books. What bliss! To be left in peace with Cordelia, Regan, Goneril and Lear himself – characters more real than my family back home or my schoolmates downstairs. The rhythm! The story! The magical words! What happiness! What comfort!

All too soon, I heard a smattering of footsteps approaching. Were visiting hours over? Surely, it couldn't be one o'clock already!

I heard the voices of Irene Tan and Eleanor Lui. They were trying on new dresses, hairbands and ribbons, chuckling at their reflections in the full-length bathroom mirror.

'What a stunning outfit!' Irene was exclaiming. 'Do you dare go into lunch wearing this skimpy little number after what happened this morning at breakfast?'

'That was almost too close for comfort!' Eleanor replied.

'Why did you do it anyway?'

'I thought Adeline might *like* an egg for breakfast once in a while. My number is 31 and hers is 37. Mama is always bringing me eggs on Sundays even though I tell her not to. I can't *stand* eating them, especially the way they soft-boil them here, with the yolk all runny. Reminds me of snot. Yesterday I wrapped a half-eaten egg in my paper napkin and trashed it in the wastebasket in the study when no one was looking. Unfortunately Ma-Mien [Horse-face] Mother Valentino came across it and fished it out. At first I denied it was mine, but she merely pointed to the number on the shell. "It's a *sin* to waste food like this when so many of your countrymen are starving to death!" she screamed. Then she forced me to get a spoon and eat it. Later in the day, I sneaked into the kitchen and changed the number on my egg from one to seven. Thought Adeline might get a kick out of having her number called for a change! How was *I* to know she hates eggs! All I'm aware of is that she gets neither eggs nor visitors on Sundays.'

'They say Adeline is brilliant but, to me, she's rather pathetic too. Rushing around in that infantile brown dress looking like a refugee fresh off a junk from the mainland. Never gets any letters either; though she's always first in line when mail gets delivered. I heard Monica say to her yesterday, "Expecting a letter from someone? I wouldn't hold my breath if I were you!"'

'Monica is just unhappy she and Adeline will be in the same class next term after the holidays. No "brain" likes to be upstaged. In spite of how she dresses, I think Adeline will be okay eventually. She has a sort of special spirit and it's a person's inner core that counts, don't you think?'

The lunch-bell sounded and they scurried off. I waited a while longer, then opened the door a crack to make sure no one was around. Whew! What a relief! The coast was finally clear!

In the bathroom mirror I stared at myself while washing my hands, full of inarticulate emotion. I mulled over Eleanor's secret attempt to pass on her unwanted egg for me to consume, thinking, Who am I kidding? The whole world knows of my 'eggless state' and some even feel sorry for me. No way will I ever allow myself to be the object of anyone's charity or pity. Besides, in spite of everything, is there not a hint of respect in their sentiments towards me?

I walked to my dormitory and sat at the edge of my bed after drawing the curtain around me for privacy, then stacked my books beside my torch in the bedside locker. Did the sisters know that I frequently read by torch under the bedclothes after 'lights-out'? Did other thirteen-year-olds also have terrifying thoughts at night and difficulty sleeping? Were they sometimes besieged by anxiety and nameless 'monsters of the deep'? If so, how did *they* deal with these paralysing fears about their future? What was *their* escape route?

I looked down with distaste at my shrunken brown dress two sizes too small ... my 'refugee costume'! Better change back into my school uniform before joining my peers for lunch, I thought. At least my uniform was the right size and still fitted me.

19. End of Term
學 期 到 終

I T WAS the last day of term. Classes had finished and we boarders sat in the lounge waiting for our parents to take us home for the summer holidays.

Eleanor Lui was wearing her 'good' shoes with the two-inch heels, examining herself in the mirror and fluffing up her hair.

'I must admit my bangs are rather nice . . . even if I say so myself,' she announced.

'They certainly look better than your legs!' replied Monica unkindly, thereby drawing attention to her own slim, well-shod feet. It was true that Eleanor's legs did appear somewhat fat and beefy in comparison as she tottered around unsteadily on her high heels.

'The problem is I love to eat too much,' Eleanor said candidly with a giggle. 'Remember yesterday when we had a discussion on crocodiles in Ma-mien Valentino's science class? I was wondering how barbecued crocodile meat would taste when Ma-mien suddenly asked me whether crocodiles have lungs. As long as their meat tastes good, who cares how they breathe?'

'That's why you are such a marvellous cook!' her loyal friend Irene Tan exclaimed. 'Everything is reduced to a recipe in your head. Do you remember that discussion we had in English class on the word "serendipity"?'

We all burst out laughing. Our English teacher, Mother Louisa, had just defined the meaning of 'serendipity' as 'a discovery by accident of things which one is not in search of'.

'Now, girls, I want you to give me some examples to illustrate this word and make it come alive for the class,' she instructed.

Rachel raised her hand. 'How about the discovery of America by Columbus? He was looking for a shortcut to the East Indies when he came upon a whole new continent.'

'Very good indeed! Another example, girls?'

'Last Sunday my dad was telling me about the Korean War,' Daisy Chen said. 'He read in the newspapers that many badly wounded American soldiers were being saved by this medicine called penicillin. Ten years ago they would all have died. Apparently an English doctor in London called Alexander Fleming dropped some mould on a plate of germs and noticed how all the germs around the mould got killed. That's how he discovered penicillin. Completely by accident!'

'This is another excellent example. Now, do you remember last week's lesson on the word galvanism? Can we combine the two concepts: serendipity and galvanism?'

The week before, Mother Louisa had said that the word galvanism came from an Italian man named Luigi Galvani who first noticed a frog's leg-muscle twitching when its nerve was stimulated. However, no one knew the answer to the question because she hadn't mentioned what Mr Galvani was doing with the frog's leg to begin with when he made his discovery.

'Eleanor!' Mother Louisa finally asked. 'Wake up! Do you have a theory? What is the story about Mr Galvani and his frogs?'

'Oh! Mother Louisa!' gushed Eleanor enthusiastically. 'Frogs' legs are delicious stir-fried with a little ginger and soya sauce. So tender and juicy. In my dad's restaurant, we have frogs' legs and I order them every time. Only they're called "field chickens" on the menu. Same thing really.' She paused briefly and must have suddenly remembered to whom she was speaking. 'I think Mr Galvani was eating frogs' legs for dinner. Maybe he bit on a nerve by mistake and the leg twitched or something. That's another example of serendipity.'

Mother Louisa arched her eyebrows while the whole class roared. 'Amazing! So you have Mr Galvani chewing on a bunch of twitching frogs' legs!' She waited for the uproar to die down, then continued, 'In actual fact, Mr Galvani was hanging frogs' legs by a copper wire from an iron railing at his home. A gust of wind blew the copper wire against the iron railing and the frogs' legs twitched. Without meaning to, he had accidentally created an electric current. This serendipitous event in the eighteenth century resulted in the discovery of galvanism.'

One by one my fellow boarders left, calling out 'best wishes' and 'happy summer holidays' to each other. Eventually, only Rachel Yu, Mary Suen and I were left behind.

Though I felt a special closeness to these two friends, I was never able to openly confide in them anything about my family. Those were emotions I repressed and hated to even think about, let alone express. Besides, they had their own problems.

Mary's father kept a 'small wife' and spent most of his time with his second family. Her mother, though ostensibly his 'big wife', only saw him on Mary's birthday and Chinese New Year. Neglected and ignored, Mrs Suen became bitter and quarrelsome. On the rare occasions when he did come 'home', he and Mary's mother argued constantly.

Rachel's parents were separated. Her father, a well-known jockey and horse-trainer, saved every penny to keep her at Sacred Heart. She was his sole reason for existence and an investment for his future but she felt smothered by his expectations.

After the hubbub and excitement of everyone's departure, I developed a stinging headache. Even though I had mentioned nothing of my summer plans, all the girls knew I was again the only boarder not going home for the holidays because I had not bothered to pack. It was hard to be the only one left behind time after time and I couldn't help feeling sorry for myself. Mary and Rachel were probably staying around deliberately for as long as possible to keep me company. Did they sense my mood?

I sauntered out onto the balcony and they followed me. It was getting dark and lights were coming on all the way down the slope, across Victoria Harbor and into the peninsula. We could see the giant ships dotting the bay below, and well-lit ferry boats moving smoothly to and fro between Hong Kong and Kowloon. I was seized by a longing to escape.

'More than anything,' I told them, 'I yearn to grow up, get out of here and see the world. Wouldn't it be wonderful if the three of us could sail away together on one of the big boats down there to all those countries we've been reading about: Japan, England, Australia, America? We must get away, stand on our own two feet and create our own destiny.'

'Let's make a pact,' Rachel said, 'that we'll always be there for each other, wherever we may be.'

Solemnly, the three of us placed our six hands on top of one another's and made a giant fist.

20. Pneumonia
肺 炎

MY HEADACHE worsened after Mary and Rachel went home and I was left alone. All night long I tossed and turned, feeling hot one minute and cold the next, trying to find a comfortable position. There was a tickle in my throat and I couldn't stop coughing.

Next morning, the sight of my breakfast sickened me. It was very depressing to sit in the refectory all by myself, filled with a feeling of *déjà vu*. In the middle of it I had a coughing fit and ended up vomiting. When I came back from the bathroom, I coughed up some blood.

Mother Mary felt my forehead and told me I was burning up. She ordered me to go to bed and called a doctor. My temperature shot up to 104 degrees. When the doctor came, he immediately admitted me to the hospital.

While I was hospitalised, Mary Suen came to see me every day. She was my one and only visitor. Her mother lived within walking distance of the hospital and Mary told me she had nothing better to do. On one occasion Father dropped in; Mary saw him because she happened to come into my room while he was leaving. Later, she was able to report to our friends that not only did I actually have a father, but he was also handsome, well dressed and looked 'very important'; thus disproving once and for all the widely held suspicion that I was an orphan.

The doctors injected me with penicillin and I recovered. Father's chauffeur came to fetch me when I was discharged. To my amazement, instead of taking me directly back to school, he drove towards the car ferry terminal instead.

'Am I going home?' I asked, half hopeful and half fearful.

'Yes. Those are your mother's orders.'

Third Brother opened the door when I rang the bell. He had recently arrived from Shanghai. I was overjoyed to see him and had a million questions.

'Where *is* everyone? The flat is so quiet!'

'Father is at the office. Niang, Fourth Brother and Little Sister have been invited to a friend's house. Before Niang left, I heard her tell the chauffeur to bring you home so you can recuperate here for one week.'

I was greatly relieved. 'So it's just the three of us for the time being. Where is Ye Ye?'

'He is having lunch. Let's join him. I've been waiting for you.'

We found Ye Ye sitting by himself in the dining-room, despondently staring at his plate. On it were some steamed carrots, a small piece of poached fish, a mound of rice and a few potatoes. His face lit up when I ran to his side and greeted him. 'Ye Ye!'

'Ah, Wu Mei! You're home. I must apologise for not waiting for you to have lunch. My diabetes is worse and this English doctor friend of your father's has put me on this special diet.' He looked down with distaste at his food. 'I have to eat punctually at eight, noon and six. Otherwise my blood-sugar goes sky-high. The trouble is, I get so tired of eating the same thing three times a day every day.'

He sounded so sad I felt like crying. Instead I sat down beside him to keep him company and asked Third Brother, 'How is Aunt Baba?'

'She's fine. Still working at Grand Aunt's bank. She keeps worrying about you and Ye Ye.'

'Did the Communists bother you?'

'No. Life in Shanghai is better than ever. Actually,' he lowered his voice, 'I was having such a good time I didn't want to come to Hong Kong at all. Big Brother and Second Brother left over a year ago to go to university in England. So at home it was just Aunt Baba and me. She treated me like a king!'

'Life in Shanghai won't be like that forever!' Ye Ye warned. 'The Communists will show their true colours sooner or later. Besides, your father has plans for you to study in England next year. Just like your two older brothers.'

'How lucky! Oh! If only I could go to university in England too! I'd give anything in the world to be able to do that! Alas! It's not for us girls.' A thought struck me and I continued, 'Where is Big Sister? Is she still in Taiwan?'

'No! Against everyone's advice, she went back to Tianjin with her husband and took their baby daughter with them. Yes! Big Sister is now a mother and I have my first great-granddaughter,' Ye Ye replied. 'What a mistake she's making in going back to Communist China! Mark my words! She'll come to regret it.'

'What are your future plans?' Third Brother turned to me and asked. 'How are you doing at school these days?'

Before I could reply, Ye Ye said proudly, 'True to form, she continues to top her class year after year. She started in Form 1 when she first came to Hong Kong. The next year, she skipped a grade and attended Form 3. We just received a letter from Mother Superior saying that they're encouraging her to skip another grade. In September she'll be going into Form 5; and she's only thirteen years old.'

'Not bad!' Third Brother exclaimed. 'You must feel pretty good about yourself.'

'Oh, I don't know. What good does it do? Being top of my class and skipping grades and all that. My friends probably think I'm some sort of freak: reading all the time. Not that it'll get me anywhere.

They nicknamed me "scholar" but I don't know whether that's complimentary or derogatory. I read because I have to. It drives everything else from my mind. It lets me escape to find other worlds. The people in my books become more real than anyone else. They make me forget.'

'It's not so bad here, is it?' Third Brother asked wistfully.

'How can you say that!' I exclaimed. 'But then you've only just arrived. Besides, you're a son, not a despised daughter, and you have England to look forward to. For me, it's bad. In fact, very bad. To begin with, I have no future. I'm terrified they'll force me into an arranged marriage like Big Sister's just to be rid of me. I don't know what they have in store, but you can be sure it's not England. I've been here for over two years and this is only the third time I've been allowed home. The rest of the time I'm shut away behind convent doors like a nun. Last time I was home was six months ago at Chinese New Year's. I was helping Little Sister with her homework when Niang pointedly told her not to spend too much time with me and sent her away. Who needs it? No one. She treats me like a leper, and I know she doesn't like me. Quite honestly, I don't like myself either. As for Father, he doesn't even remember my name. In his mind, I'm nothing. Less than nothing. A piece of garbage to be thrown out –'

'Don't talk like that!' Ye Ye interrupted. 'You mustn't talk like that! You have your whole life ahead of you. Everything is possible! I've tried to tell you over and over that far from being garbage, you are precious and special. Being top of your class merely confirms this. But you can vanquish the demons only when you yourself are convinced of your own worth.

'The world is changing. You must rely on yourself and not end up married off like Big Sister. I have faith in you. Go out there and dare to compete in the most difficult examinations. Create your own destiny! Your Ye Ye is an old man now and his days are numbered. Who knows how long we have to talk like this? But no matter what happens, always remember that my hopes are with you. Trust me! Continue to work hard! One day you'll show the world what you are really made of.'

At that moment Ah Gum entered the room with our lunch. In contrast to Ye Ye's spartan repast, she placed sweet and sour spare ribs, string beans with beef in black bean sauce and sautéed spinach on the table for Third Brother and me. As soon as she left the room, Ye Ye quickly served himself a generous helping of ribs.

'I know I'm not supposed to eat this,' he said, 'and your father will probably yell at me should he find out. But my doctor has taken all the taste out of my food. Sometimes I ask myself, What's the point of hanging on if I can't even enjoy my meals? What else is there left for me?'

There was so much despair in his voice it made me cringe. I longed desperately to make it up to him and ease his pain. So I said, 'When I go back to school, I'll try even harder. And if I should be so lucky as to succeed one day, it'll be because you believed in me.'

21. Play-writing Competition
戲 劇 比 賽

WHEN I went back to school after one
week, the holidays were not yet over and
all the girls were still home with their families.
The place was a tomb.

Day after day, I sat in the library reading and
chatting with Mother Louisa, who also served as
the school librarian. In one magazine, I came
across the announcement of a play-writing
competition open to English-speaking children
anywhere in the world. Inspired by Ye Ye's
exhortations, I approached Mother Louisa with
some trepidation.

'Should I enter this competition? Do you think
I stand a chance?'

'As good a chance as anyone else. Since you have time on your hands and wish to enter, why don't you try? It will focus your energies and give you a goal.'

'Because I don't think I'm that talented. I'm afraid of losing.'

'Look at it this way. Anyone who enters has a chance. However, if you don't enter, then you certainly will have destroyed your chance before you even begin. First, you must believe that you can do anything you set your mind to. Remember the old adage, genius is ten per cent inspiration, ninety per cent perspiration.'

I sent for information and was tremendously excited when I received the application form as well as four pages of extremely complicated rules and regulations by return post. That was the only mail I ever got during my entire time at Sacred Heart. Laboriously, I read and reread the instructions and set to work. I called my play *Gone with the Locusts* and created the story of an imaginary little African girl who was stolen from her parents by bandits during a famine brought on by locusts. Into her lips, I injected my loneliness, isolation and feelings of being unwanted. To my heroine, I gave everything of myself. What began as a diversion became a passion. In the end, I had her triumph over her adversities through her own efforts. I enjoyed my task so much that I was almost sorry when it was completed.

'This play is dedicated to my grandfather', I wrote proudly on the cover sheet and sent it off the day before the girls came back from vacation.

School restarted and I was in the fifth form. Though I wrote many letters to Father and Niang begging them to allow me to go to university in England with Third Brother, they never replied. In fact, they seemed to have forgotten me entirely. When they moved into a bigger house, I was never told but discovered it by serendipity. I was helping Mother Mary sort out a bulky pile of incoming mail addressed to the sisters during Christmas vacation. To my amazement, I came across a card sent by my parents! Besides holiday greetings, Joseph and Jeanne Yen informed the nuns of their change of address. Instead of Boundary Street in Kowloon, they were living on Stubbs Road in Hong Kong. Of course, they had not thought it necessary or worthwhile to write to me.

Chinese New Year's came and went in 1952 without any contact from home. There was also no news about my play even though six months had gone by.

Mother Louisa consoled me. 'Be patient. No news is good news. As long as you don't hear, you can keep on hoping. Pray hard. Miracles do happen.'

'If I win, will you help me inform my Ye Ye? He'll be so pleased! He really believes in me and I dedicated my play to him.'

March, 1952

I was playing basketball and the score was close. I lowered my head and lunged towards the basket, eluding my defender by suddenly switching to her left. I found myself free and took careful aim . . .

'Adeline!'

Ma-mien Valentino was calling me. I shot the ball anyway and watched its arc as it sailed through the air and through the hoop. Swish! Two points! The score was tied. For once I didn't miss.

'Adeline! Come here at once!'

'Aw, Mother! Can we please finish our game? Five more minutes? Please . . . ?'

'No, Adeline! This can't wait. Your chauffeur is waiting for you downstairs to take you home.'

'My chauffeur? Am I hearing correctly? Take me home? Have I died and gone to heaven?' There was a hush and all the girls on the basketball court were listening, with their faces upturned. I knew what was going through their minds because I was thinking the same thing. 'Adeline actually has a chauffeur?' We were all equally astonished!

I left the court and ran to Mother Valentino. 'Go wash your hands and comb your hair,' she said. 'There is no time for you to change clothes. Your father has sent his chauffeur to take you directly to the Buddhist Temple. Your grandfather has died. Today is his funeral.'

I sobbed throughout the long ceremony, besieged by sorrow and loss. No one else was crying. Father, Niang, Third Brother, Fourth Brother and Little Sister sat stony-faced next to me as the monks chanted endless prayers and extolled Ye Ye's virtues. The heady smell of incense permeated the air.

Between masses of white flowers I saw my Ye Ye's kind, sad face peering out at me from his photograph perched on his coffin. I heard his voice once more, exhorting me to try my best and create a life of my own. It was because of him that I had dared to enter the play-writing competition. Now he would never know how much he had influenced me. Did anyone else in the world care whether I won or lost?

I saw Niang looking at me with open disdain as we filed out and waited for Father's chauffeur to drive us home. I knew I looked ghastly with my dirty school uniform, scuffed tennis shoes, straight unpermed hair, bitten fingernails and swollen eyes red from crying. Standing beside her made me feel especially worthless, plain and small. I caught a whiff of her perfume and was sick with fear.

As the Studebaker approached, Niang turned to Father and announced in a loud voice that I was looking uglier and uglier as I grew older and taller. Hearing this, Fourth Brother gave a snort of contempt. Oh, the misery of it all! I felt as if I was being skinned alive.

At home, Niang called me into the living-room. She instructed me to look for a job when school ended that summer because Father had too many children to support and could no longer 'afford' my school fees. She reminded me that I was fourteen years old and could not expect to live in luxury at the expense of Father forever.

After lunch, the chauffeur brought me back to school. It was the free interval after tea and my fellow boarders were playing a game.

Rachel screamed out, 'Join us! What in your opinion is your best physical, intellectual or social feature, Adeline? Each player first writes her own notion on a sheet of paper. The rest of us then put down their views for comparison.'

As we progressed, it was illuminating to see how differently my friends viewed themselves and one another. One by one, without realising it, we each revealed our inner beings.

We went down the list alphabetically. Daisy (Style vs Sincerity). Eleanor (Hair vs Lips). Mary (Legs vs Hands). Irene (Eyes vs Friendliness). Rachel (Intelligence vs Generosity).

Because I came in late, I was allowed to go last. It was my turn. My paper remained blank as I thought desperately, Do I have *any* redeeming features?

'Come on, Adeline!' Rachel prompted. 'Write something!'

'Okay!' I finally blurted out. 'Here it is!'

Rachel opened my paper, 'What's this? You wrote "nothing". What does that mean?'

'That's right! Nothing! I don't think any of my features are good. That's what I mean.'

'And that's your honest opinion of yourself?' Rachel asked.

'Yes! That's it. Everything is ugly. I loathe myself.'

'Well, we beg to differ. In fact, we have voted you most likely to succeed.'

The combination of Ye Ye's sudden death and Niang's undisguised disdain sent me into a horrible depression. Night after night, I was unable to sleep – worried about my future, wondering what was to become of me. I spent hours praying in the hushed solemnity of the school chapel, trying to figure a way out. I dreamt of running away and sneaking back into mainland China, rejoining Aunt Baba and my schoolfriends in Shanghai. I wrote numerous beseeching letters to my parents, begging them to let me go to England, where my two oldest brothers were studying. 'Third Brother is leaving for London in August,' I wrote. 'May I please accompany him? I do so yearn to go to university. I have skipped two grades in the last three years and am still top of my class. I know I'm only a girl and don't deserve it, but will you please be so kind? I promise I'll pay you back as soon as I graduate and get a decent job.'

During the days I was unable to eat, but spent hours gazing at the harbour below, dreaming of a time when I could board one of those ships anchored in the bay and sail away to fabulous institutions of learning far, far from home.

Every afternoon at tea-time I waited in line when mail was distributed, hoping for a letter from home. It was a standing joke among the girls that I was always there waiting, though I had only received one single letter in my three years at the school. Not from home but from the play-writing board. Still, I couldn't help being there every day.

The idea of leaving school forever in a few months enveloped me in a constant state of gloom. Without the prospect of furthering my education, my dreams were withering and I was in agony. Day after day, anxiety spun its web around my thoughts and spread to all corners of my heart.

Time went by relentlessly and it was Saturday again. Eight weeks more and it would be the end of term ... in my case perhaps the end of school forever.

Four of us were playing Monopoly. My heart was not in it and I was losing steadily. Outside it was hot and there was a warm wind blowing. The radio warned of a possible typhoon the next day. It was my turn and I threw the dice. As I played, the thought of leaving school throbbed at the back of my mind like a persistent toothache.

'Adeline!' Ma-mien Valentino was calling.

'You can't go now,' Mary protested. 'For once I'm winning. One, two, three, four. Good! You've landed on my property. Thirty-five dollars, please. Oh, good afternoon, Mother Valentino!'

We all stood up and greeted her.

'Adeline, didn't you hear me call you? Hurry up downstairs! Your chauffeur is waiting to take you home!'

Full of foreboding, I ran downstairs as in a nightmare, wondering who had died this time. Father's chauffeur assured me everyone was healthy.

'Then why are you taking me home?' I asked.

'How should *I* know?' he answered defensively, shrugging his shoulders. 'Your guess is as good as mine. They give the orders and I carry them out.'

During the short drive home, my heart was full of dread and I wondered what I had done wrong. Our car stopped at an elegant villa at mid-level, halfway up the hill between the peak and the harbour.

'Where are we?' I asked foolishly.

'Don't you know anything?' the chauffeur replied rudely. 'This is your new home. Your parents moved here a few months ago.'

'I had forgotten,' I said as I got out.

Ah Gum opened the door. Inside, it was quiet and cool.

'Where is everyone?'

'Your mother is out playing bridge. Your two brothers and Little Sister are sunbathing by the swimming-pool. Your father is in his room and wants to see you as soon as you get home.'

'See me in his room?' I was overwhelmed by the thought that I had been summoned by Father to enter the Holy of Holies – a place to which I had never been invited. Why? Was I to be forced into an arranged marriage?

Timidly, I knocked on the door. Father was alone, looking relaxed in his slippers and bathrobe, reading a newspaper. He smiled as I entered and I saw he was in a happy mood. I breathed a small sigh of relief at first but became uneasy again when I wondered why he was being so nice, thinking, Is this a giant ruse on his part to trick me? Dare I let my guard down?

'Sit down! Sit down!' He pointed to a chair. 'Don't look so scared. Here, take a look at this! They're writing about someone we both know, I think.'

He handed me the day's newspaper and there, in one corner, I saw my name ADELINE YEN in capital letters prominently displayed.

'It was announced today that 14-year-old Hong Kong schoolgirl ADELINE JUN-LING YEN of Sacred Heart Canossian School, Caine Road, Hong Kong, has won first prize in the International Play-writing Competition held in London, England, for the 1951–1952 school year. It is the first time that any local Chinese student from Hong Kong has won such a prestigious event. Besides a medal, the prize comes with a cash reward of FIFTY ENGLISH POUNDS. Our sincere congratulations, ADELINE YEN, for bringing honour to Hong Kong. We are proud of you.'

Is it possible? Am I dreaming? Me, the winner?

'I was going up the lift this morning with my friend C. Y. Tung when he showed me this article and asked me, "Is the winner Adeline Jun-ling Yen related to you? The two of you have the same uncommon last name." Now C. Y. himself has a few children about your age but so far none of them has won an international literary prize, as far as I know. So I was quite pleased to tell him you are my daughter. Well done!'

He looked radiant. For once, he was proud of me. In front of his revered colleague, C. Y. Tung, a prominent fellow businessman also from Shanghai, I had given him face. I thought, Is this the big moment I have been waiting for? My whole being vibrated with all the joy in the world. I only had to stretch out my hand to reach the stars.

'Tell me, how did you do it?' he continued. 'How come *you* won?'

'Well, the rules and regulations were so very complicated. One really has to be dedicated just to understand what they want. Perhaps I was the only one determined enough to enter and there were no other competitors!'

He laughed approvingly. 'I doubt it very much but that's a good answer.'

'Please, Father,' I asked boldly, thinking it was now or never. 'May I go to university in England too, just like my brothers?'

'I do believe you have potential. Tell me, what would you study?'

My heart gave a giant lurch as it dawned on me that he was agreeing to let me go. How marvellous it was simply to be alive! Study? I thought. Going to England is like entering heaven. Does it matter what you do after you get to heaven?

But Father was expecting an answer. What about creative writing? After all, I had just won first prize in an international writing competition!

'I plan to study literature. I'll be a writer.'

'Writer!' he scoffed. 'You are going to starve! What language are you going to write in and who is going to read your writing? Though you may think you're an expert in both Chinese and English, your Chinese is actually rather elementary. As for your English, don't you think the native English speakers can write better than you?'

I waited in silence. I did not wish to contradict him.

'You will go to England with Third Brother this summer and you will go to medical school. After you graduate, you will specialise in obstetrics. Women will always be having babies. Women patients prefer women doctors. You will learn to deliver their babies. That's a foolproof profession for you. Don't you agree?'

Agree? Of course I agreed. Apparently, he had it all planned out. As long as he let me go to university in England, I would study anything he wished. How did that line go in Wordsworth's poem? *Bliss was it in that dawn to be alive.*

'Father, I shall go to medical school in England and become a doctor. Thank you very, very much.'

22. Letter from Aunt Baba
姑 媽 來 信

22 September, 1952

My precious little treasure,

What a surprise to hear from you after four long years and to learn that you are on your way with Third Brother to study in Oxford, England. Your letter (post-marked Singapore) gave me more happiness than anything else in the world. The only thing better would be a personal visit from you. Thank you for thinking of me on your long ocean voyage. What an adventure for the two of you!

Here in Shanghai, I share your father's big house on Avenue Joffre with Miss Chien and two maids. I am tired this evening after my usual long day's work at the Women's

*Bank. However, I have so much in my heart to say to you
that I must write to you tonight.*

*I must confess that I have been much worried about you
since we have been apart. Before he passed away in March
this year, Ye Ye used to write and give me news of you. I
knew Aunt Reine had taken you from Tianjin to Hong
Kong and that you were in boarding-school there. In his last
letter to me, Ye Ye was gravely concerned about your future.
That is why it is such a pleasant surprise to learn that your
father has agreed to send you for further studies in England.*

*Tonight I miss Ye Ye more than ever and that is another
reason why I am writing. Some day, you will be my age
and may wish to speak to me but I may no longer be around.
Keep in mind always, always, no matter what, that you are
worthwhile and very important to me, wherever I may be.*

*When you were little and things were going badly, you
used to run to me and ask me to take away this 'big, black
cloud' in your head, do you remember? I'd tell you a story
and you would fall asleep listening. Here is a new story I
want you never to forget. Whenever you feel discouraged,
and those clouds come back, take out this letter and read it
again. It is a message from your Aunt Baba, who will
always hold you precious in her heart.*

*This story was told to me by my own mother (your Nai
Nai) many years before she passed away. It is part of our
Chinese folklore.*

Once upon a time, there was a little girl called Ye Xian 葉限 who lived during the Tang dynasty in China. Her father had two wives and two daughters, one by each wife. Ye Xian's mother died, followed by her father. Her stepmother maltreated her, showing preference for her own daughter.

Ye Xian was a talented potter and spent her time at the wheel perfecting her skill. People came from far and wide to purchase her pots. Her only friend was a goldfish which she loved. Her stepmother became jealous, caught the fish and ate it, hiding the fishbones under a pile of manure. Ye Xian found the bones and hid them in her room. The presence of the fishbones gave off magical rays which imparted a special sheen to her pots.

A Great Festival was being held but Ye Xian was forbidden by her stepmother to attend. After her stepmother and sister left, Ye Xian dressed herself in a beautiful cloak of kingfisher feathers and a pair of gold shoes which were light and elegant.

At the festival she spoke briefly to the local warlord who was much struck by her beauty. Her stepmother recognised her and gave chase. Ye Xian ran home but lost one of her shoes, which was found by the warlord. He ordered all the girls in his kingdom to try it on, but it was too small. The cobbler who made the shoes came forward and told the war-lord of Ye Xian,

who had traded one of her pots for the gold shoes.
Through her own talent and effort, Ye Xian had
bought the shoes which led eventually to marriage
with the war-lord. They lived happily ever after.

In England and America, your Grand Aunt tells me there is
a similar story called Cinderella. In a way, both Ye Xian
and Cinderella are like you: children who are mourning for
their dead mothers. Their stories may be perceived as
talismans against despair.

By winning that prestigious international play-writing
competition, you have climbed another rung on the ladder
of success. Like Ye Xian, you have defied the odds and
garnered triumph through your own efforts. Your future is
limitless and I shall always be proud of you,

my Chinese Cinderella.

The Story of Ye 葉 Xian 限: The Original Chinese Cinderella

FOLLOWING this is the Chinese text of a story written during the Tang Dynasty (AD 618–906). It is the story of Ye Xian 葉限, also known as the original Chinese Cinderella. Isn't it mind-boggling to think that this well-loved fairy-tale was already known over one thousand years ago?* My Aunt Baba told me about Ye Xian when I was fourteen years old, and you can read all about her in Chapter 22.

---

* Paper was invented in China in the year AD 105 by Tsai Lun, a Han Dynasty eunuch who served as an official in the imperial court. A book of Buddhist scriptures printed in the year AD 868 (Tang Dynasty) was discovered by Sir Aurel Stein in 1907. Considered the world's first complete printed book, it is preserved in the British Museum and is apparently in perfect condition.

I am grateful to Feelie Lee PhD and Professor David Schaberg of the East Asian Languages & Culture Department, University of California at Los Angeles, for their scholarship and research in finding the book *Yu Yang Za Zu* at UCLA's East Asian Library. *Yu Yang Za Zu* contains a miscellany of ninth-century Chinese folk-tales, among them the Chinese text of Ye Xian's story. The author's name was Duan Cheng-shi 段成式, and the stories were collected in an encyclopedic book that went through many editions during the last eleven hundred years.

Please note the absence of punctuation, and the beautiful Chinese characters. This is how ancient classic Chinese texts were written. The oldest Chinese books were copied by hand.

For many years the story of Cinderella was thought to have arisen in Italy in 1634. Iona and Peter Opie in *The Classic Fairy-tales*, published by Oxford University Press in 1974, consider the Italian Cinderella story to be the oldest European version. We now realise that Duan Cheng-shi's Ye Xian predates the Italian tale by eight hundred years. Cinderella seems to have travelled to Europe from China. Perhaps Marco Polo brought her from Beijing to Venice eight hundred years ago. Who knows?

葉限

南人相傳秦漢前有洞主吳氏土人呼為吳洞娶
兩妻一妻卒有女名葉限少惠善淘金父愛之末
歲父卒為後母所苦常令樵險汲深時嘗得一鱗
二寸餘赬鰭金目遂潛養於盆水中日長易數器
大不能受乃投於後池中女所得餘食輒沉以食
之女至池魚必露首枕岸他人至不復出其母知
之每伺之魚未嘗見也因詐女曰爾無勞乎吾為
爾新其襦乃易其弊衣後令汲於他泉計里數百
也母徐衣其女衣袖利刀行向池呼魚魚即出首
因斫殺之魚已長丈餘膳其肉味倍常魚藏其骨
於郁樓之下逾日女至向池不復見魚矣乃哭於
野忽有人披髮粗衣自天而降慰女曰爾無哭爾
母殺爾魚矣骨在糞下爾歸可取魚骨藏於室所
須第祈之當隨爾也女用其言金璣衣食隨欲而
具及洞節母往令女守庭果女伺母行遠亦往衣
翠紡上衣躡金履母所生女認之謂母曰此甚似
姊也母亦疑之女覺遽反遂遺一隻履為洞人所

得母歸但見女抱庭樹眠亦不之慮其洞鄰海島
島中有國名陀汗兵強王數十島水界數千里洞
人遂貨其履於陀汗國國主得之命其左右履之
足小者履減一寸乃令一國婦人履之竟無一稱
者其輕如毛履石無聲陀汗王意其洞人以非道
得之遂禁錮而拷掠之竟不知所從來乃以是履
棄之於道旁即遍歷人家捕之若有女履者捕之
以告陀汗王怪之乃搜其室得葉限令履之而信
葉限因衣翠紡衣躡履而進色若天人也始具事
於王載魚骨與葉限俱還國其母及女即為飛石
擊死洞人哀之埋於石坑命曰懊女塚洞人以為
媒祀求女必應陀汗王至國以葉限為上婦一年
王貪求祈於魚骨寶玉無限逾年不復應王乃葬
魚骨於海岸用珠百斛藏之以金為際至徵卒叛
時將發以贍軍一夕為海潮所淪成式舊家人李
士元所說士元本邑州洞中人多記得南中怪事

Historical Note

CHINA is a big country roughly the size of the USA. It has the world's oldest continuous civilisation and Chinese writing has remained virtually unchanged for the last three thousand years.

Until the middle of the nineteenth century, China was the most powerful country in Asia. The country looked inward and considered herself the centre of the world, calling herself 中國 *zhong guo*, which means central country.

In 1842, China lost the Opium War. As a result, Britain took over Hong Kong and Kowloon. For about one hundred years afterwards, China suffered many humiliating defeats at the hands of all the major industrial powers, including Britain, France and Japan. Many port cities on China's coast (such as Tianjin and Shanghai) fell under foreign control. Native Chinese were ruled by foreigners and lived as second-class citizens in their own cities.

In 1911, there was a revolution and the imperial Manchu court in Beijing was abolished. Sun Yat-sen became president and proclaimed China a republic. However, the country broke into fiefdoms ruled by war-lords who fought each other for the control of China. Chiang Kai-shek, a military general and protégé of Sun Yat-sen, took over after Sun's death in 1925.

Japan first seized Taiwan from China in 1895. She then usurped Manchuria. In July 1937, she declared war on China and quickly occupied Beijing and Tianjin.

When I was born in November 1937 in Tianjin, the city was still divided into foreign Concessions. However, outside the Concessions, the Japanese were in charge. My family lived in the French Concession, where we were ruled by French citizens under French law. My sister and I attended a French missionary school and were taught by French Catholic nuns.

On December 7, 1941, Japan bombed Pearl Harbor and declared war on the USA and Britain. On the same day, Japanese troops marched into Tianjin's foreign Concessions. Because my father did not wish to collaborate with the Japanese, he took an assumed name and escaped from Tianjin to Shanghai. We joined him there two years later.

In 1945, Japan surrendered, and the Second World War was at an end. Chiang Kai-shek was back in charge. His triumph was short-lived because a civil war soon erupted between the Nationalists under Chiang and the Communists under Mao Ze-dong.

In 1948, during the height of the civil war, my parents took me from Shanghai back to Tianjin while they themselves went back to Shanghai, and then on to Hong Kong. The Communists won the war and drove the Nationalists out of mainland China to Taiwan.

I was the only student left in my school when the Communists commandeered Tianjin. All the other students had escaped. Luckily, I was rescued by an aunt who took me out of school and brought me to Hong Kong.

At that time, Hong Kong was still a British colony and my parents sent me to another Catholic boarding-school. They themselves were hoping that the Americans would help Chiang Kai-shek take back mainland China. The Korean War broke out in 1950, pitching North Korea (aided by Communist China and the Soviet Union) against South Korea (aided by the United Nations). People in Hong Kong were extremely nervous that Communist China would march in from the mainland and occupy Hong Kong. This did not happen. A truce was reached instead and the Korean War ended.

I left Hong Kong in August 1952 and went to school in England.

Postscript

MY LIFE changed dramatically after I went to England. I spent three years in two different English boarding-schools, then entered University College and London Hospital Medical College. It was a wonderful period of my life. The whole world of science was opening up to me. I could not wait to get to classes every morning. Laboratory experiments reminded me of intricate chess games. My opponent was the great 'unknown', about to be unmasked. Along the way, there were tantalising clues.

After graduation I emigrated to California, USA, and practised as a physician for twenty-six years. Although by then I was very happily married and had two lovely children, I still yearned for my parents' acceptance. My father died in 1988 but our stepmother Niang prevented us from reading his original will. It seemed as if I would never know if my father had ever wanted me.

Two years later, Niang herself passed away. It was then that Third Brother suddenly informed me that I had been unexpectedly and mysteriously left out of our stepmother's will. I also found out that there had been a conspiracy to hide the truth from me. This discovery, together with my desperate search for my father's missing will, was like a page torn out of my childhood, when I had been so cruelly punished for speaking out against Niang. Forty years later, it was happening all over again.

You can read all about it in my autobiography, *Falling Leaves*, which was first published in London in 1997 by Michael Joseph and Penguin Books.

I hope you have enjoyed reading *Chinese Cinderella*.

Extra!

Extra!

READ ALL ABOUT IT!

ADELINE YEN MAH

CHINESE
CINDERELLA

1937 *Born 30 November in Tianjin, China, the youngest of five siblings. Soon after, Adeline's mother dies*

1938 *When Adeline is a year old, her father remarries and has two more children*

1948 *The family move to Hong Kong and Adeline attends the Sacred Heart School where she is top of the class*

1951 *Wins an international play-writing competition for her play* Gone with the Locusts *and her father allows her to study in England*

1952 *Leaves Hong Kong for boarding school in England*

1955 *Studies medicine at University College and London Hospital Medical School in England*

1960 *Graduates as a physician*

1964 *Emigrates to the USA and works as an anaesthesiologist at West Anaheim Community Hospital in California, USA, and becomes chief of anaesthesia*

1972 *Marries artist Robert A. Mah*

1974 *Adeline and Robert's daughter Ann is born*

1997 *Adeline's autobiography,* Falling Leaves, *is published and becomes an international bestseller*

1999 Chinese Cinderella: The Secret Story of an Unwanted Daughter, *her autobiography for children, is published*

2000 Chinese Cinderella *receives the Children's Literature Council of Southern California's award for Compelling Autobiography*

2001 Watching the Tree, *a book of Chinese philosophy, is published*

2002 *Her fourth adult book,* A Thousand Pieces of Gold: A Memoir of China's Past through its Proverbs, *is published*

2004 Chinese Cinderella and the Secret Dragon Society, *an adventure story for children based on a true story Adeline wrote when she was only ten years old, is published*

2008 China, Land of Dragons and Emperors, *a history of China for teenagers, is published. Establishes 'Chinese Character a Day' website where she teaches Mandarin Chinese for free*

2009 *A further children's adventure,* Chinese Cinderella and the Mystery of the Song Dynasty Painting, *is published*

2010 *Establishes the Falling Leaves Foundation to promote understanding between the East and the West and provide funds for the study of Chinese history, language, and culture*

2013 *Creates PinYinPal, a free digital word-game app to learn Chinese*

2015 *Lives in California and London. Over the last two years, Adeline has been developing free, digital word-game apps to teach Chinese over the internet on iPads and iPhones. Please visit her website ChineseCharacterADay.com to find out more about PinYinPal and Chinese Gems*

INTERESTING FACTS

Adeline's father did not record the date of her birth and instead gave her his own birthday of 30 November. This was a common practice before the establishment of the People's Republic of China in 1949.

Adeline's Chinese name is: Yen Jun-ling

'Falling leaves return to their roots' is a Chinese proverb which means to go back to one's origin.

WHERE DID THE STORY COME FROM?

Adeline Yen Mah wrote Chinese Cinderella *after the successful publication of her first autobiography,* Falling Leaves, *which details the years of Adeline's life from fourteen years of age into adulthood. Adeline felt compelled to write about her early childhood, to preserve her memories through her writing, and she dedicated her story to all unwanted children all over the world.*

ADELINE SAYS:
'Although *Chinese Cinderella* was written when I was in my late 50s, inside I am still the same little child yearning for the love of my parents.'

GUESS WHO?

A   'This will teach you to favour your duck over mine!'

B   She took the key from a gold chain around her neck and placed my certificate under her jade bracelet . . .

C   'How sneaky you all are to get money from Ye Ye without your father's knowledge!'

D   'I'm in a restaurant. I got lost when I tried to walk home from school.'

E   'True to form, she continues to top her class year after year.'

ANSWERS: A) *Second Brother* B) *Aunt Baba* C) *Niang* D) *Jun-ling* E) *Ye Ye*

WORDS
GLORIOUS
WORDS!

Lots of words have several different meanings – here are a few you'll find in this Puffin book. Use a **dictionary** or look them up online to find other definitions.

alacrity *brisk, cheerful readiness to do something*

catechism *a summary of the principles of Christian religion, in the form of questions and answers, used for teaching*

euphoric *an intense feeling of happiness*

inadvertently *unintentionally*

mah-jong *a Chinese game played with small tiles*

Quel dommage! *A French phrase meaning 'What a shame!'*

rickshaw *a small, two-wheeled covered vehicle pulled by a person*

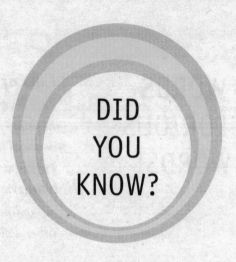

DID YOU KNOW?

Until the early 1900s China was a **male dominated** society. Women had **no rights** and marriages were arranged with **no say** about it from the women.

Women with **small feet** were considered more attractive and suitable for marriage than women with big feet. When a girl was about three years old, her mother would tightly wrap her feet in a bandage, even though it was **extremely painful** and very unhealthy, to prevent her feet from growing normally. The practice of **foot binding** was almost gone by the time Communist leader **Mao Tse-Tung** became China's leader in 1949.

Variants on the theme of **Cinderella** are known all around the world: the Chinese version, **The Story of Ye Xian**, is dated around AD 850.

QUIZ

Thinking caps on – *let's see how much you can remember! Answers are at the bottom of the next page. (No peeking!)*

1 *How many siblings does Wu Mei have?*

a) *Two*

b) *Four*

c) *Five*

d) *Six*

2 *What name do the children give to Niang's private rooms?*

a) *Heavenly Kingdom*

b) *Sacred Hill Top*

c) *Holy of Holies*

d) *House of Kings*

3 How does Third Brother comfort Wu Mei
after the death of PLT?

a) He brings her some flowers

b) He promises to buy her another duckling

c) He attends the funeral

d) He gives her a hug

4 How does Wu Mei react when Niang beats
baby Susan?

a) She runs away

b) She cries out for her to stop

c) She remains silent

d) She pushes Niang out of the way

5 After Wu Mei wins the writing competition,
where does she beg her father to let her study?

a) England

b) America

c) Canada

d) France

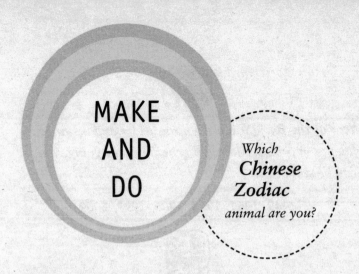

MAKE
AND
DO

Which
Chinese
Zodiac
animal are you?

According to the Chinese Zodiac calendar, each year is named after a different animal – twelve animals in all. The Chinese New Year is between late January and early February and this is when the next animal year starts.

Adeline Yen Mah was born in the Year of the Ox. Find the year of your birth in the list below to discover what animal you are in the Chinese Zodiac, and some of your characteristics!

Year of the Rat *(You are imaginative, charming and generous. You work hard to achieve your goals, and are a perfectionist.)*

1948, 1960, 1972, 1984, 1996, 2008

Year of the Ox *(You are a born leader and inspire con-fidence in others. Although generally easy-going, you can be stubborn.)*

1949, 1961, 1973, 1985, 1997, 2009

Year of the Tiger *(You are sensitive, emotional and loving. You are a deep-thinker, and courageous. But you can be short-tempered.)*

1950, 1962, 1974, 1986, 1998, 2010

Year of the Hare *(You are talented and affectionate, and admired and trusted by others.)*

1951, 1963, 1975, 1987, 1999, 2011

Year of the Dragon *(You are energetic, popular and fun-loving. You are also honest, sensitive and brave.)*

1952, 1964, 1976, 1988, 2000, 2012

Year of the Snake *(You are sympathetic and try to help those less fortunate. Although you are calm on the surface, you are intense and determined in whatever you do.)*

1953, 1965, 1977, 1989, 2001, 2013

Year of the Horse *(You are popular, quick-witted and adventurous. You are wise and perceptive, but can be impatient.)*

1954, 1966, 1978, 1990, 2002, 2014

Year of the Sheep *(You are creative, artistic and gentle. You strongly believe in what you do, but you can be pessimistic.)*

1955, 1967, 1979, 1991, 2003, 2015

Year of the Monkey   *(You are clever, skilful and lots of fun. You are good at making decisions but can quickly become despondent.)*

1956, 1968, 1980, 1992, 2004, 2016

Year of the Rooster   *(You like to be busy, are devoted to work and skilled at what you do. You are a little eccentric, outspoken and sometimes selfish.)*

1957, 1969, 1981, 1993, 2005

Year of the Dog   *(You are born to succeed. You are loyal, honest and intelligent, and inspire confidence in others, but you can be sharp-tongued.)*

1958, 1970, 1982, 1994, 2006

Year of the Pig   *(You are reliable and extremely loyal. You are quick-tempered but you don't like to argue.)*

1959, 1971, 1983, 1995, 2007

IN THIS YEAR

1999
Fact Pack

What else was happening in the world when this Puffin book was published?

The **Millennium Dome** opens in London.

The famous illustrator **Quentin Blake** becomes the first ever **Children's Laureate**.

The world population reaches **six billion!**

The European Union **introduces the Euro** currency.

PUFFIN
WRITING
TIP

Adeline says: Keep a **diary** *and write something in it every day, including* **book reviews***. The* **more** *you write, the* **better** *your writing will be.*

A Puffin Book can take you to amazing places.

WHERE WILL YOU GO?

#PackAPuffin

HOW MANY HAVE YOU READ?

stories that last a lifetime

Animal tales

- [ ] The Trumpet of the Swan
- [ ] Gobbolino
- [ ] Tarka the Otter
- [ ] Watership Down
- [ ] A Dog So Small

War stories

- [ ] Goodnight Mister Tom
- [ ] Back Home
- [ ] Carrie's War

Magical adventures

- [ ] The Neverending Story
- [ ] Mrs Frisby and the Rats of NIMH
- [ ] A Wrinkle in Time

Unusual friends

- [ ] Stig of the Dump
- [ ] Stuart Little
- [ ] The Borrowers
- [ ] Charlotte's Web
- [ ] The Cay

Real life

- [ ] Roll of Thunder, Hear My Cry
- [ ] The Family from One End Street
- [ ] Annie
- [ ] Smith

stories that last a lifetime

Ever wanted a friend who could take you to magical realms, talk to animals or help you survive a shipwreck? Well, you'll find them all in the **A PUFFIN BOOK** collection.

A PUFFIN BOOK will stay with you **forever**. Maybe you'll read it again and again, or perhaps years from now you'll suddenly **remember** the moment it made you **laugh** or **cry** or simply see things **differently**. Adventurers **big** and **small**, rebels out to **change** their world, even a mouse with a **dream** and a spider who can spell – these are the characters who make **stories** that last a **lifetime**.

Whether you love animal tales, war stories or want to know what it was like growing up in a different time and place, the **A PUFFIN BOOK** collection has a story for you – you just need to decide where you want to go next . . .